First Workshop on Metaphor in NLP

(Meta4NLP 2013)

Atlanta, Georgia, USA
13 June 2013

ISBN: 978-1-62748-996-6

Printed from e-media with permission by:

Curran Associates, Inc.
57 Morehouse Lane
Red Hook, NY 12571

CURRAN ASSOCIATES INC.
proceedings.com

Some format issues inherent in the e-media version may also appear in this print version.

Printed by Curran Associates, Inc. (2013)

For permission requests, please contact the Association for Computational Linguistics at the address below.

Association for Computational Linguistics
209 N. Eighth Street
Stroudsburg, Pennsylvania 18360

Phone: 1-570-476-8006
Fax: 1-570-476-0860

acl@aclweb.org

Additional copies of this publication are available from:

Curran Associates, Inc.
57 Morehouse Lane
Red Hook, NY 12571 USA
Phone: 845-758-0400
Fax: 845-758-2634
Email: curran@proceedings.com
Web: www.proceedings.com

Meta4NLP 2013

The First Workshop on Metaphor in NLP

Proceedings of the Workshop

13 June 2013
Atlanta, GA, USA

Introduction

Characteristic to all areas of human activity (from poetic to ordinary to scientific) and, thus, to all types of discourse, metaphor becomes an important problem for natural language processing. Its ubiquity in language has been established in a number of corpus studies and the role it plays in human reasoning has been confirmed in psychological experiments. This makes metaphor an important research area for computational and cognitive linguistics, and its automatic identification and interpretation indispensable for any semantics-oriented NLP application.

The work on metaphor in NLP and AI started in the 1980s, providing us with a wealth of ideas on the structure and mechanisms of the phenomenon. The last decade witnessed a technological leap in natural language computation, whereby manually crafted rules gradually give way to more robust corpus-based statistical methods. This is also the case for metaphor research. In the recent years, the problem of metaphor modeling has been steadily gaining interest within the NLP community, with a growing number of approaches exploiting statistical techniques. Compared to more traditional approaches based on hand-coded knowledge, these more recent methods tend to have a wider coverage, as well as be more efficient, accurate and robust. However, even the statistical metaphor processing approaches so far often focused on a limited domain or a subset of phenomena. At the same time, recent work on computational lexical semantics and lexical acquisition techniques, as well as a wide range of NLP methods applying machine learning to open-domain semantic tasks, open many new avenues for creation of large-scale robust tools for recognition and interpretation of metaphor.

This workshop is the first one focused on modelling of metaphor using NLP techniques. Recent related events include workshops on Computational Approaches to Figurative Language (NAACL 2007) and on Computational Approaches to Linguistic Creativity (NAACL 2009, NAACL 2010). We received 14 submissions and accepted 10. Each paper was carefully reviewed by at least 3 members of the Program Committee. The selected papers offer explorations into the following directions: (1) creation of metaphor-annotated datasets; (2) identification of new features that are useful for metaphor identification; (3) cross-lingual metaphor identification.

The papers represent a variety of approaches to utilization and creation of datasets. While existing annotated corpora were used in some papers (Dunn, Tsvetkov et al), most papers describe creation of new annotated materials. Along with annotation guidelines adapted from the MIP and MIPVU procedures (Badryzlova et al), more intuitive annotation protocols are explored in Beigman Klebanov and Flor, Hovy et al, Heintz et al, Mohler et al, and Strzalkowski et al.

The papers present a number of novel and extended features for metaphor detection. Topic models, abstractness/concreteness, and semantic classifications based on an ontology are each used in multiple papers. Additional features include classes of named entities (Tsvetkov et al), WordNet examples and glosses (Wilks et al); suggestive evidence is presented regarding potential usefulness of a relationality feature (Jamrozik et al). A distinguishing characteristic of multiple submissions is the interest in cross-lingual approaches to metaphor identification. Accordingly, contributors explore features that can be supported by resources that exist in languages like Russian, Spanish, and Farsi (Strzalkowski et al., Tsvetkov et al, Heintz et al).

The program of the workshop also features two invited talks that complement the discussion by addressing topics that are not addressed by this year's submissions, namely, the relationship between metaphor and action (Srini Narayanan), and interpretation of metaphors (John Barnden).

We wish to thank everyone who showed interest and submitted a paper, all of the authors for their contributions, the members of the Program Committee for their thoughtful reviews, the invited speakers for sharing their perspectives on the topic, and all the attendees of the workshop. All of these factors contribute to a truly enriching event!

Workshop co-chairs:
Ekaterina Shutova, University of California at Berkeley, USA
Beata Beigman Klebanov, Educational Testing Service, USA
Joel Tetreault, Nuance, USA
Zornitsa Kozareva, USC Information Sciences Institute, USA

Organizers:

Ekaterina Shutova, University of California, Berkeley, USA
Beata Beigman Klebanov, Educational Testing Service, USA
Joel Tetreault, Nuance, USA
Zornitsa Kozareva, USC Information Sciences Institute, USA

Program Committee:

Shlomo Argamon, Illinois Institute of Technology, USA
John Barnden, University of Birmingham, UK
Gemma Boleda, University of Texas at Austin, USA
Danushka Bollegala, University of Tokyo, Japan
Marisa Boston, Nuance, USA
David Bracewell, LCC, USA
Ted Briscoe, University of Cambridge, UK
Jaime Carbonell, CMU, USA
Stephen Clark, University of Cambridge, UK
Paul Cook, University of Melbourne, Australia
Gerard de Melo, University of California at Berkeley, USA
Alice Deignan, Leeds University, UK
Afsaneh Fazly, University of Toronto, Canada
Anna Feldman, Montclair State University, USA
Jerry Feldman, University of California at Berkeley, USA
Michael Flor, Educational Testing Service, USA
Marjorie Freedman, BBN, USA
Deidre Gentner, Northwestern University, USA
Yanfen Hao, Electronics Industry Research Institute, ShanXi, China
Jerry Hobbs, University of Southern California, USA
Eugenie Giesbrecht, Karlsruhe Institute of Technology, Germany
Valia Kordoni, Humboldt University Berlin, Germany
Anna Korhonen, University of Cambridge, UK
George Lakoff, University of California at Berkeley, USA
Alex Lascarides, University of Edinburgh, UK
Mark Lee, University of Birmingham, UK
Patricia Lichtenstein, University of California, Merced, USA
Katja Markert, University of Leeds, UK
James H. Martin,University of Colorado at Boulder, USA
Andreas Musolff, University of East Anglia, UK
Srini Narayanan, University of California at Berkeley, USA
Malvina Nissim, University of Bologna, Italy
Diarmuid Ó Séaghdha, University of Cambridge, UK
Gerard Steen, VU Amsterdam, The Netherlands

Thierry Poibeau, Ecole Normale Superieure and CNRS, France
Caroline Sporleder, Saarland University, Germany
Carlo Strapparava, Fondazione Bruno Kessler, Italy
Tomek Strzalkowski, SUNY Albany, USA
Marc Tomlinson, LCC, USA
Oren Tsur, Hebrew University, Israel
Peter Turney, National Research Council Canada, Canada
Tim van de Cruys, IRIT and CNRS, Toulouse, France
Tony Veale, Korean Advanced Institute for Science and Technology, Republic of Korea
Aline Villavicencio, Federal University of Rio Grande do Sul, Brazil and MIT, USA
Andreas Vlachos, University of Cambridge, UK
Yorick Wilks, Florida Institute of Human and Machine Cognition, USA

Invited Speakers:

Srini Narayanan, University of California, Berkeley, USA
John Barnden, University of Birmingham, UK

Table of Contents

Workshop Program

Thursday, June 13, 2013

9:00–9:10	Opening remarks
9:10–10:05	Invited talk: Srini Narayanan "From Metaphor to Action"
10:05–10:30	*What metaphor identification systems can tell us about metaphor-in-language* Jonathan Dunn
10:30–11:00	Coffee break
11:00–11:25	*Argumentation-Relevant Metaphors in Test-Taker Essays* Beata Beigman Klebanov and Michael Flor
11:25–11:45	*Relational words have high metaphoric potential* Anja Jamrozik, Eyal Sagi, Micah Goldwater and Dedre Gentner
11:45–12:10	*Semantic Signatures for Example-Based Linguistic Metaphor Detection* Michael Mohler, David Bracewell, Marc Tomlinson and David Hinote
12:10–13:40	Lunch
13:40–14:20	Invited talk: John Barnden "Computational Approaches to Metaphor Interpretation: Some Considerations arising from a Deep Reasoning System"
14:20–14:45	*Automatic Metaphor Detection using Large-Scale Lexical Resources and Conventional Metaphor Extraction* Yorick Wilks, Adam Dalton, James Allen and Lucian Galescu
14:45–15:10	*Cross-Lingual Metaphor Detection Using Common Semantic Features* Yulia Tsvetkov, Elena Mukomel and Anatole Gershman
15:10–15:30	*Identifying Metaphorical Word Use with Tree Kernels* Dirk Hovy, Shashank Shrivastava, Sujay Kumar Jauhar, Mrinmaya Sachan, Kartik Goyal, Huying Li, Whitney Sanders and Eduard Hovy
15:30–16:00	Coffee break
16:00–16:25	*Automatic Extraction of Linguistic Metaphors with LDA Topic Modeling* Ilana Heintz, Ryan Gabbard, Mahesh Srivastava, Dave Barner, Donald Black, Marjorie Friedman and Ralph Weischedel

Thursday, June 13, 2013 (continued)

16:25–16:50 *Robust Extraction of Metaphor from Novel Data*
Tomek Strzalkowski, George Aaron Broadwell, Sarah Taylor, Laurie Feldman, Samira Shaikh, Ting Liu, Boris Yamrom, Kit Cho, Umit Boz, Ignacio Cases and Kyle Elliot

16:50–17:15 *Annotating a Russian corpus of conceptual metaphor: a bottom-up approach*
Yulia Badryzlova, Natalia Shekhtman, Yekaterina Isaeva and Ruslan Kerimov

17:15–17:30 Closing remarks

What metaphor identification systems can tell us about metaphor-in-language

Jonathan Dunn
Purdue University
West Lafayette, Indiana USA
jonathan.edwin.dunn@gmail.com

Abstract

This paper evaluates four metaphor identification systems on the 200,000 word VU Amsterdam Metaphor Corpus, comparing results by genre and by sub-class of metaphor. The paper then compares the rate of agreement between the systems for each genre and sub-class. Each of the identification systems is based, explicitly or implicitly, on a theory of metaphor which hypothesizes that certain properties are essential to metaphor-in-language. The goal of this paper is to see what the success or failure of these systems can tell us about the essential properties of metaphor-in-language. The success of the identification systems varies significantly across genres and sub-classes of metaphor. At the same time, the different systems achieve similar success rates on each even though they show low agreement among themselves. This is taken to be evidence that there are several sub-types of metaphor-in-language and that the ideal metaphor identification system will first define these sub-types and then model the linguistic properties which can distinguish these sub-types from one another and from non-metaphors.

1 Introduction

The purpose of this paper is to evaluate four systems for identifying metaphor-in-language on the large and representative VU Amsterdam Metaphor Corpus (Steen, et al., 2010) and then to analyze the correct and incorrect identifications in order to see what they can tell us about the linguistic properties of metaphor-in-language. The four metaphor identification systems include a word-level semantic similarity measurement method (Sporleder and Li, 2009; Li and Sporleder, 2010), a word-level abstractness measurement method (Turney and Littmann, 2003; Turney, et al., 2011), a grammatical-relation-level source-target mapping method (Shutova, 2010; Shutova and Teufel, 2010; Shutova, Sun, and Korhonen, 2010; Shutova, Teufel, and Korhonen, 2013), and an utterance-level domain interaction method (Dunn, 2013b).

2 The VU Amsterdam Metaphor Corpus

The VU Amsterdam Metaphor Corpus (Steen, et al., 2010) consists of approximately 200,000 words taken from the British National Corpus's Baby Corpus and divided into four genres: academic, news, fiction, and conversation. It was manually annotated for metaphoric uses of words by five analysts using a version of the MIP method (Pragglejaz Group, 2007). For the purposes of this study, the corpus was divided into sentences, under the assumption that each sentence represents an utterance. There are 16,202 sentences in the corpus. Sentences which contain at least one metaphoric use of a word are labeled as metaphoric sentences. This is done because a metaphorically used word is not metaphoric except in relation to its linguistic context; thus, a larger linguistic unit like the sentence is necessary for revealing metaphorically used words.

The VU Amsterdam Corpus is annotated with several sub-classes of metaphor-in-language. The sub-classes included in this evaluation are MRW-Met (a metaphoric use of a metaphor related word);

Table 1: Number of sentences with sufficient representation in each system.

System	Non-Metaphor	MRW-Met	MRW-Lit	PP	Double	WIDLII
Total	7,979	5,977	126	754	180	1,186
Similarity	4,300	4,274	104	612	153	855
Abstractness	6,851	5,497	118	723	174	1,090
Source-Target	6,256	5,391	121	719	178	1,070
Domain Interaction	6,770	5,588	122	729	178	1,115

MRW-Lit (a literal use of a metaphor related word); PP (a possible personification resulting in a metaphor related word); Double (a metaphor related word which is involved in a double metaphor; for example, personification and a conceptual metaphor); WIDLII (possible metaphor related words which were considered ambiguous between metaphoric and non-metaphoric use).

Table 1 shows a break-down of the number of sentences in each of these sub-classes in the corpus as a whole and as represented by each of the metaphor identification systems. Because each system uses different linguistic properties to identify metaphor-in-language and uses different methods to represent those properties, the systems differ in how many of the sentences are sufficiently represented. For example, the semantic similarity measurement system looks at pairwise similarity values while the abstractness measurement system looks at values for individual words. Thus, the abstractness system could potentially have twice as many data points as the similarity system. The numbers in Table 1 include only the sentences with a minimum number of data points. The evaluation results below do not take into account sentences for which a system has insufficient representation. However, it is important to note that the systems differ in how many sentences they adequately represent, which means that some (for example, the similarity system) are less able to identify metaphor-in-language because they have a less robust representation of the linguistic utterance.

For the purposes of this study, metaphor identification was conceptualized as a sentence-level task. For example, the systems evaluated here could be used within a larger computational semantic system to separate metaphoric and non-metaphoric sentences for purposes of reasoning. One result of this choice is that some of the original systems need to be slightly reconceptualized; thus, it is better to say that these systems are inspired by the cited systems, rather than strict reimplementations of those systems. The similarity and abstractness systems originally were meant to decide which uses of a given verb are metaphoric and which are not metaphoric. In the present study, however, metaphor is not limited to verbs and the systems do not know which words in the sentence may be metaphoric (e.g., it could be any noun or any verb, etc.). Thus, these systems have been altered to determine whether there are any metaphorically used words anywhere in the sentence. Further, all of the reconceptualized systems compared here involve training or seed metaphors, even those which were originally unsupervised systems.

3 Identifying Metaphor-in-Language Using Semantic Similarity

The semantic similarity system (Sporleder and Li, 2009; Li and Sporleder, 2010) uses pairwise semantic similarity to detect metaphoric uses of words. As conceptualized in this study, the system is designed to detect whether any of the words in the sentence are used metaphorically without knowing in advance which words are candidates for metaphoric use.

While the original system used Normalized Google Distance (Cilibrasi and Vitanyi, 2007) to measure semantic similarity, the evaluation in this study used Iosif's SemSim system (Iosif and Potamianos, 2012). There were two main reasons for not using the NGD measure: (1) SemSim offers more control because the corpus used to determine pairwise similarity is known and can be made similar to the test corpus; (2) SemSim is more transparent in terms of its methodology and its results are more stable over time. For this evaluation we used the Open American National Corpus (henceforth,

OANC (Ide and Suderman, 2004)), which consists of 14 million words taken from spoken and written contemporary American English, to determine the pairwise similarity values. Both the test corpus and OANC were lemmatized and had common function words removed. Pairwise similarities were determined for all words in the test corpus which occurred 10 or more times, for a total of 1,691 words. SemSim's contextual window was set at 2. As with all systems discussed below, Morpha (Guido, Carroll, and Pearce, 2001) was used for lemmatization and OpenNLP (Apache, 2011) was used for named entity recognition.

The variables used in the original system had to be changed slightly because no particular word in the sentence is given a special focus. The following variables were used: (1) the number of similarity measurements for a given sentence; (2) the average similarity; (3) the standard deviation of similarity, in order to see how much divergence there was from the average; (4) the highest pairwise similarity; (5) the lowest pairwise similarity; (6) the difference between the highest and lowest pairwise similarity. One of the weaknesses of this particular implementation of the system is that it only considers words that are adjacent to one another (with function words removed). While the original system also used the average pairwise similarity between the candidate word and all other words, this was not possible here given that there were no words starting as candidates.

4 Identifying Metaphor-in-Language Using Word Abstractness

The word abstractness system uses a measurement of word abstractness to identify highly abstract contexts which are posited to be more likely to contain metaphors. In the reconceptualization of the system evaluated here there is also a focus on disparities in abstractness ratings within a given sentence, so that the mixture of abstract and concrete words can be used to detect possible metaphors.

The system first rates lexical items according to how abstract they are, on a scale from 0 to 1, with 1 being the most abstract. The approach to rating abstraction is taken from (Turney, et al., 2011); a list of rated lexical items is available from the authors. The system tags the words in the sentence with their parts of speech and finds the abstractness rating for each; if an abstractness rating is not available for a particular word form, the system attempts to find a match for its lemmatized form. All words not found on the list of abstractness ratings after these searches were removed.

For each sentence a feature vector was created that consisted of twelve different combinations of abstractness ratings: (1) the number of abstractness ratings available for the sentence; (2) the average abstractness for all words; (3) the standard deviation of the abstractness for all words; (3)-(4) the average and standard deviation for the abstractness of nouns; (5)-(6) the average and standard deviation for the abstractness of verbs; (7)-(8) the average and standard deviation for the abstractness of adjectives and adverbs; (9)-(10) the highest and lowest abstractness in the sentence; (11) the difference between the highest and lowest abstractness; (12) the difference between the average abstractness for nouns and for verbs. Empty slots in the feature vector (e.g., if there were no adjectives) were filled with a value of 0.5 for abstractness, following the original system.

5 Identifying Metaphor-in-Language Using Source-Target Mappings

The source-target mapping system clusters verbs and nouns using their distributional properties and argues that abstract nouns will cluster according to the metaphoric source domains to which they are connected. The system moves from the linguistic utterance to the underlying conceptual mapping by assuming that the verb directly represents the source domain in the metaphoric mapping and that nouns (functioning as the subject and/or object of the verb) directly represent the target. Thus, the system looks at grammatical relations containing a verb and a noun and generalizes from seed metaphors to other metaphors involving words from the same clusters.

The first part of evaluating the source-target mapping approach to metaphor identification was to cluster lexical items. The method for clustering verbs is described in (Sun and Korhonen, 2009); (Sun, Korhonen, and Krymolowski, 2008) provide a resource of the most frequent 1,510 English verbs in the Gigaword corpus divided into 170 clusters.

These clusters were used in the evaluation. The procedure used for clustering nouns in (Shutova, Teufel, and Korhonen, 2013) is to include the frequency of grammatical relations (subject, object, indirect object), as annotated by the RASP parser, in a feature vector. In evaluating the source-target system, we took a different approach to obtaining noun clusters. Starting with 8,752 nouns examined by Iosif's SemSim system (Iosif and Potamianos, 2012), we used a pairwise similarity matrix (measured using the Google-based Semantic Relatedness metric, as computed by Iosif) for the feature vector used for clustering nouns. The nouns were divided into 200 clusters using Weka's (Witten and Frank, 2005) implementation of the k-means algorithm.

The search for metaphors was performed on the RASP-parsed version of the evaluation corpus. A total of 1,000 randomly selected metaphoric sentences were used as seed metaphors; any relation between two different clusters was accepted as a candidate. Many of the seed metaphoric utterances contained multiple grammatically related clusters (e.g., verb-object) which were candidates for the metaphoric material in the utterance. In this evaluation we have erred on the side of inclusion by searching for all possible candidates. A total of 903 grammatical relations between clusters were identified in the seed sentences; no attempt was made to trim this number down. While the original system removed verbs which have loose selectional restrictions, such verbs were not removed from the clusters here; the original system focuses on preventing false positives, but in the evaluation here the focus is on preventing false negatives, which such a reduction would necessarily create.

6 Identifying Metaphor-in-Language Using Domain Interactions

The domain interaction system (Dunn, 2013b) is a knowledge-based system unlike the previous distributional-semantic systems. It identifies metaphoric utterances using properties of the concepts pointed to by lexical items in the utterance. The system has two stages: first, determining what concepts are present in an utterance and what their properties are; second, using these properties to model metaphor.

The system maps lexical items to their WordNet synsets (WordNet, 2011) using the part of speech tags to maintain a four-way distinction between nouns, verbs, adjectives, and adverbs. The system then maps the WordNet synsets onto concepts in the SUMO ontology (Niles and Pease, 2001) using the mappings provided (Niles and Pease, 2003). This is done using the assumption that each lexical item is used in its default sense, so that no disambiguation takes place. Once the concepts present in the utterance have been identified in this manner, using the concepts present in the SUMO ontology, the system uses domain (ABSTRACT, PHYSICAL, SOCIAL, MENTAL) and event-status (PROCESS, STATE, OBJECT) properties of each concept present in the utterance. These are not present as such in the SUMO ontology, but were developed following Ontological Semantics (Nirenburg and Raskin, 2004) as a knowledge-base specific to the system.

The domain interaction system was implemented with a feature vector created using the properties of the concepts referred to by lexical items in the utterance. The feature vector uses the following variables: (1) number of concepts in the utterance; (2-5) number of instances of each type of domain (ABSTRACT, PHYSICAL, SOCIAL, MENTAL); (6-8) number of instances of each type of event status (PROCESS, STATE, OBJECT); (9) number of instances of the domain with the highest number of instances; (10) number of instances of event-status with the highest number of instances; (11) sum of the individual domain variables minus (9); (12) sum of individual event-status variables minus (10); (13) number of domain types present at least once in the utterance; (14) number of event-status types present at least once in the utterance; (15) number of instances of the main domain divided by the number of concepts; (16) number of other domain instances divided by the number of concepts; (17) number of main event-status instances divided by the number of concepts; (18) number of other event-status instances divided by the number of concepts.

7 Evaluation Results

The evaluation results discussed in this section consider only the sentences for which each system has the minimum representation; for example, the se-

Table 2: Results for each system across all genres and sub-classes.

System	True Positive	False Positive	True Negative	False Negative	F-Measure
Similarity	5,936	4,214	86	62	0.444
Abstractness	4,627	3,049	3,752	2,954	0.582
Source-Target	1,063	785	5,470	5,496	0.440
Domain Interaction	5,446	3,664	3,106	2,286	0.583

Table 3: Results for each system across all genres and sub-classes without Named Entity Recognition.

System	True Pos.	False Pos.	True Neg.	False Neg.	F-Meas.	Represented
Similarity	5,658	3,973	63	56	0.444	9,750
Abstractness	5,882	4,205	441	354	0.482	10,883
Source-Target	1,725	1,342	2,171	2,677	0.487	8,547
Domain Interaction	6,561	4,205	1,462	676	0.573	12,904

mantic similarity system had a minimum representation for many fewer sentences than does the abstractness system, but those unrepresented sentences are not held against the system. Three of the systems use feature vectors: the semantic similarity, word abstractness, and domain interaction systems. To make the evaluation comparable all three systems are evaluated using Weka's (Witten and Frank, 2005) implementation of the logistic regression algorithm, following (Turney, et al., 2011), using cross-validation (100 folds) and a ridge estimator value of 0.2. The evaluation of the source-target system searched for the 903 seed relations in the RASP-parsed test corpus. The sentences used as seeds were removed from the test corpus before searching. For each evaluation, the reported F-Measure is the weighted average of the F-Measures for metaphors and non-metaphors.

Table 2 shows the evaluation results for the four systems on the entire corpus. The similarity system has the highest number of true positives (5,936), but also the highest number of false positives (4,214). In fact, the similarity system identifies very few utterances as non-metaphors and this makes the results rather unhelpful. The abstractness and domain interaction systems have similar F-measures (0.582 and 0.583, respectively); both make a large number of predictions for both metaphor and non-metaphor, so that they attempt to distinguish between the two, but these predictions are not particularly accurate. The source-target system stands out here, as it does below, with a significantly smaller number of false positives than the other systems (785). At the same time, it also has a significantly higher number of false negatives (5,496). The similarity and source-target systems are on opposite ends of the spectrum in terms of over-identifying and under-identifying metaphor-in-language, and both have similar F-measures (0.444 and 0.440, respectively) which are lower than the abstractness and domain interaction systems.

In Table 3 the same results across all genres and sub-types are presented for implementations without Named Entity Recognition. The only system which performs significantly differently is the abstractness system, with an F-Measure of 0.482 without vs. 0.582 with NER. This decline goes hand-in-hand with the fact that the system with NER has sufficient representation for a total of 14,454 sentences, while without NER it has sufficient representation for only 10,883 sentences.

Table 4 starts to break these results down further by genre, in order to find out if the systems perform differently on different sorts of texts. Every system except for the similarity system (with F-measures of 0.444 and then 0.463) performs more poorly on fiction than on the corpus as a whole. More interestingly, within the fiction genre the similarity and abstractness systems do not predict that any utterances are non-metaphors, which makes their F-measures largely meaningless. The source-target system continues to make a distinction between metaphor and

Table 4: Results for each system in the Fiction genre.

System	True Positive	False Positive	True Negative	False Negative	F-Measure
Similarity	1,778	1,135	0	0	0.463
Abstractness	2,074	1,375	0	0	0.452
Source-Target	293	244	1,151	1,567	0.379
Domain Interaction	2,067	1,349	75	67	0.485

Table 5: Results for each system in the News genre.

System	True Positive	False Positive	True Negative	False Negative	F-Measure
Similarity	1,806	292	0	0	0.796
Abstractness	1,940	321	0	0	0.792
Source-Target	348	61	262	1,352	0.321
Domain Interaction	1,956	324	0	0	0.792

non-metaphor within this genre, although the true and false positives (293 and 243, respectively) are much closer to one another than when looking at the corpus as a whole.

Table 5 looks at the systems' performance within the News genre. The similarity system, which above made few predictions for non-metaphor continues to predict only metaphors; the abstractness and domain interaction systems join it, predicting only metaphors. The source-target system, on the other hand, maintains a small number of false positives (61), although continuing to show a large number of false negatives (1,352). In terms of practical applications, the F-measures here do not adequately reflect the fact that three of the four systems essentially fail on this genre. One of the difficulties is the fact that the News genre contains 1,708 metaphoric sentences and 325 non-metaphoric sentences according to the manual annotations in the VU Amsterdam Metaphor Corpus; that means that 84% of the sentences are annotated as metaphoric.

Table 6 looks at the results within the Academic genre. Here all systems make a distinction between metaphor and non-metaphor; this is the first set on which the similarity system has predicted a meaningful number of non-metaphors. The source-target system misses the most metaphors (1,321) but also makes significantly fewer false positives (146 vs. the next lowest 590 by the similarity system). The F-measures do not adequately reflect the performance of the systems for this genre.

Table 7 shows the results within the Conversation genre. This is the reverse of the News genre: three of the four systems make no predictions of metaphors. This genre contains 1,958 utterances with at least one metaphorically used word and 5,262 without. Further, this genre contains many more short and/or fragmentary sentences than the others. Even the source-target system, which is the only system to identify any metaphors, has more than twice as many false positives as true positives (334 vs. 136, respectively), which reverses its performance on the three previous genres.

The initial conclusions we can draw from the genre break-down is that (1) the F-measure does not always reflect meaningful performance and thus that the numbers of true and false positives and negatives should be reported as well; and (2) that the performance on the corpus as a whole disguises a large amount of variation according to genre.

Table 8 shows the results for only the MRW-Met sub-class in the corpus. This is the basic metaphor sub-class in the corpus and the most common. The systems perform better on this sub-class than on any other. Interestingly, the source-target system makes more false than true positives here (785 vs. 749) and is the only system to make more false than true positives for this sub-class. It also makes more false negatives than the other systems, although the abstractness, source-target, and domain interaction systems make a comparable number (3,971 and 3,990 and 3,386, respectively). The domain interaction system

Table 6: Results for each system in the Academic genre.

System	True Positive	False Positive	True Negative	False Negative	F-Measure
Similarity	1,287	590	289	214	0.635
Abstractness	1,604	667	273	204	0.649
Source-Target	286	146	786	1,321	0.367
Domain Interaction	1,720	720	232	154	0.646

Table 7: Results for each system in the Conversation genre.

System	True Positive	False Positive	True Negative	False Negative	F-Measure
Similarity	0	0	1,994	913	0.558
Abstractness	0	0	4,165	1,759	0.580
Source-Target	136	334	3,271	1,256	0.621
Domain Interaction	0	0	4,070	1,768	0.573

makes the most true positives, although all the F-measures are comparable (the lowest is only 0.062 below the highest).

Table 9 shows the results for the ambiguous metaphors, under the label WIDLII, and the results are comparable to the results for all other sub-classes except for the MRW-Met sub-class (thus, the other sub-classes will not be discussed individually). The similarity, abstractness, and domain interaction systems do not detect any of these sentences as containing metaphorically used words. In some ways this failure is acceptable because the original analysts were not convinced that these utterances contained metaphors in the first place. The source-target system has a very uncharacteristic performance on this sub-class, with 5-times as many false positives as true positives (785 vs. 157, respectively).

This is interesting because it is exactly the opposite of the other systems, which do not predict any sentences to be metaphors at all. This difference is likely a result of the fact that the other three systems rely on feature vectors that were trained on the WIDLII / Non-Metaphor distinction, while the source-target system uses seed grammatical relations from other sub-classes as well (it shouldn't matter because the relations are hypothesized to represent conceptual metaphors for which the sub-class distinction is not relevant; more seed metaphors were not used because this would have removed them from the evaluation). In other words, the sub-class comparisons try to distinguish between WIDLII metaphors and non-metaphors in the corpus. The source-target system was trained on one and only one set of seed metaphors; in other cases this fact increased the system's performance, but in this case it had the opposite effect. It also shows that non-metaphors are more likely to contain the seed clusters than are ambiguous metaphors.

8 Error Analysis

The next question to ask is whether these four systems succeed and fail on the same metaphors. Each system makes different assumptions and is based on a different theory of what linguistic properties are essential to metaphor-in-language, and thus can be used to distinguish metaphor from non-metaphor.

Table 10: Agreement among the four metaphor identification systems using Fleiss' Kappa.

Sub-set	Full	Reduced
Fiction	0.293	0.301
News	0.279	0.277
Academic	0.282	0.286
Conversation	0.259	0.286
MRW-Met	0.280	0.291
MRW-Lit	0.285	0.298
PP	0.293	0.290
Double	0.346	0.369
WIDLII	0.278	0.292

Table 10 shows the agreement between the four

Table 8: Results for each system in the MRW-Met Sub-Class.

System	True Positive	False Positive	True Negative	False Negative	F-Measure
Similarity	2,141	1,841	2,459	2,133	0.536
Abstractness	1,505	1,287	5,514	3,971	0.537
Source-Target	749	785	5,470	3,990	0.499
Domain Interaction	2,202	1,895	4,875	3,386	0.561

Table 9: Results for each system in the WIDLII Sub-Class.

System	True Positive	False Positive	True Negative	False Negative	F-Measure
Similarity	0	0	4,300	855	0.759
Abstractness	0	2	6,799	1,090	0.798
Source-Target	157	785	5,470	768	0.785
Domain Interaction	0	0	6,770	1,115	0.793

systems as measured by Fleiss' Kappa. In the first column, under "Full," the predictions used to determine agreement differ slightly from the earlier predictions because all sentences were included, even those for which a particular system lacked sufficient representation. This was done in order to make a comparison of the four systems possible (sentences without representation could not be identified as metaphors and thus defaulted to non-metaphors). The sentences used as seeds for the source-target system were removed for all systems. A possible cause for low agreement between the systems is that if one system lacks sufficient representation for a sentence, it will cause disagreement by its lack of representation. The second column, under "Reduced," shows the agreement between the four systems for only those sentences for which all systems had an adequate representation and which were not used for seed metaphors (a total of 8,887 sentences rather than the full 16,202). The results are similar, showing that the low agreement is not caused by lack of sufficient representation.

All of the divisions, whether by genre or by subclass, have a similarly low level of agreement, with a range from 0.259 to 0.293. The sub-class of Double metaphors has a higher agreement of 0.346. This low agreement is the case even though the systems have similar overall performance on these particular genres and sub-classes. In other words, even though the systems make similar numbers of correct predictions, the particular utterances for which metaphor is correctly or incorrectly predicted are not the same.

This is an important point because if all four systems succeeded and failed on the same utterances then we could say that those particular utterances were the cause of the failure and try to model the properties of those utterances. What seems to be happening is quite the opposite: each system implements a particular model of metaphor-in-language which makes specific explicit and implicit assumptions about what metaphor-in-language is and what properties are essential for distinguishing metaphoric language from non-metaphoric language. These different models seem to be succeeding on those metaphors which fall within their scope and failing on all others, which leads to disagreement in the predictions of the systems.

9 Synthesizing the Systems

Several meta-systems were constructed using the results of the four systems on the sub-set of the corpus for which each system had adequate representation (8,887 sentences). The first meta-system identified as metaphor only those sentences which the two top-performing systems, the source-target mapping and the domain interaction systems, agreed were metaphoric; the second only those sentences which all four systems agreed were metaphoric; the third only those sentences which a majority of systems agreed were metaphoric; the fourth those sentences for which either the domain interaction or

Table 11: Results for meta-systems across all sentences with sufficient representation for all systems.

System	True Positive	False Positive	True Negative	False Negative	F-Measure
Only top two agree	520	360	3,558	4,449	0.362
Only all agree	374	244	3,674	4,595	0.341
Majority vote	1,513	1,655	2,263	2,921	0.445
Top two inclusive	3,200	2,552	1,366	1,769	0.505
Top two, settled inc	2,689	2,164	1,754	2,280	0.501
Top two, settled exc	2,086	1,688	2,230	2,883	0.485

the source-target system identified as metaphor; the fifth all sentences which the domain interaction and source-target systems agreed were metaphoric, using the similarity and abstractness systems to resolve disagreement. There are two versions of this last meta-system: the inclusive version identifies disputed sentences as metaphoric if either the similarity or abstractness system does, and the exclusive version only if the two agree.

Table 11 shows the results of the evaluations of these meta-systems. The system with the fewest false positives is the one which requires four-way agreement before an utterance is identified as metaphor; however, this also has the fewest true positives. The performance of the exclusive meta-system for the top two systems has a better proportion of true to false positives, but also has an unfortunately high number of false negatives. The majority vote meta-system has more false than true positives and, thus, is not successful. The last three meta-systems differ in how they resolve disagreements between the top two systems; there is a consistent trade-off between more true positives and fewer false positives and all three have comparable F-measures.

10 What This Tells Us About Metaphor-in-Language

What can we learn about metaphor-in-language from the successes and failures of these four metaphor identification systems? First, there is a significant difference between genres. The linguistic properties which can distinguish metaphors in one genre may not apply to other genres. Or, looked at another way, different genres are more likely to contain different types of metaphors (the types of metaphor referred to here involve different sources of metaphoric meaning and are not comparable to the corpus's sub-classes).

Second, the predictions of the four systems, regardless of their accuracy, have a relatively low level of agreement. This low level of agreement is consistent across genres and sub-classes. This means that the systems are succeeding and failing on different metaphors. Each of the systems is based on a different theory of metaphor-in-language. The combination of these two facts suggests that different types of metaphor have different linguistic properties.

Most theories of metaphor conceive of it as a single and coherent phenomenon, so that the predictions of competing theories are mutually exclusive. The lack of agreement coupled with similar success rates, however, suggests that these theories of metaphor-in-language are not mutually exclusive but rather apply to different types of metaphor-in-language. If this is the case, then a more accurate model of metaphor-in-language will start by positing a number of different types of metaphor-in-language, which differ in the source of their metaphoric meaning, and then predicting what linguistic properties can be used to distinguish among these types and between them and non-metaphors.

Metaphor identification systems can be improved by focusing on two important properties of metaphor-in-language: First, metaphors are gradient, with some being much more metaphoric than others (Dunn, 2011). One problem with the systems described in this paper is that they are forced to draw an arbitrary line between two classes to represent a gradient phenomenon. Second, metaphoric expressions receive their metaphoric meaning from different sources (Dunn, 2013a). These different types of metaphor-in-language have different properties and should be modeled individually.

References

Apache. 2011. OpenNLP

Briscoe, E., Carroll, J., Watson, R. "The Second Release of the RASP System." Curran, J. (ed.) *Proceedings of COLING/ACL 2006 Interactive Presentation Sessions* 77-80 Association for Computational Linguistics Stroudsburg, PA 2006

Cilibrasi, R. and Vitanyi, P. "The Google similarity distance." *Knowledge and Data Engineering, IEEE Transactions on* 19(3): 370–383 2007

Dunn, J. "Gradient semantic intuitions of metaphoric expressions" *Metaphor & Symbol* 26(1): 53-67 2011

Dunn, J. "How linguistic structure influences and helps to predict metaphoric meaning" *Cognitive Linguistics* 24(1): 33-66 2013

Dunn, J. "Evaluating the premises and results of four metaphor identification systems." Gelbukh, A. (ed.) *Proceedings of CICLing 2013, LNCS 7816* 471-486 Springer Heidelberg 2013

Guido, M., Carroll, J., Pearce, D. "Applied morphological processing of English." *Natural Language Engineering* 7(3): 207-223 2001

Ide, N. and Suderman, K. "The American National Corpus First Release." Lino, M. Xavier, M., Ferreira, F., Costa, R., and Silva, R. (eds.) *Proceedings of LREC-2004* 1681-1684 European Language Resources Association Paris 2004

Iosif, E. and Potamianos, A. "SemSim: Resources for Normalized Semantic Similarity Computation Using Lexical Networks." Calzolari, N., Choukri, K., Declerck, T., Doan, M., Maegaard, B., Mariani, J., Odijk, J., Piperidis, S. (eds.) *Proceedings of LREC-2012* 3499-3504 European Language Resources Association Paris 2012

Li, L. and Sporleder, C. "Using Gaussian Mixture Models to Detect Figurative Language in Context." Kaplan, R., Burstein, J., Harper, M., and Penn, G. (eds.) *Proceedings of HLT-NAACL-2010* 297–300 Association for Computational Linguistics Stroudsburg, PA 2010

Niles, I. and Pease, A. "Towards a Standard Upper Ontology" Welty, C. and Barry, C. (eds.) *Proceedings of FOIS-2001* 2-9 Association for Computational Linguistics Stroudsburg, PA 2001

Niles, I. and Pease, A. "Linking Lexicons and Ontologies: Mapping WordNet to the Suggested Upper Merged Ontology." Arabnia, H. (ed) *Proceedings of IEEE Intl Conf on Inf. and Knowl. Eng. (IKE 03)* 412-416 IEEE Press New York 2003

Nirenburg, S. and Raskin, V. *Ontological Semantics* Cambridge, MA MIT Press 2004

Pragglejaz Group "MIP: A method for identifying metaphorically used words in discourse." *Metaphor and Symbol* 22(1): 139 2007

Princeton University *WordNet* 2012

Shutova, E. "Models of Metaphor in NLP." Hajiv, J., Carberry, S., Clark, S. and Nivre, J. (eds.) *Proceedings of ACL-2010* 688–697 Association for Computational Linguistics Stroudsburg, PA 2010

Shutova, E. and Teufel, S. "Metaphor corpus annotated for source – target domain mappings." Calzolari, N., Choukri, K., Maegaard, B., Mariani, J., Odijk, J., Piperidis, S., Rosner, M. and Tapias, D. (eds.) *Proceedings of LREC 2010* 3255–3261 European Language Resources Association Paris 2010

Shutova, E., Sun, L,. and Korhonen, A. "Metaphor identification using verb and noun clustering." Huang, C. and Jurafsky, D. (eds.) *Proceedings of COLING 2010* 1002–1010 Tsinghua University Press Beijing 2010

Shutova, E., Teufel, S., and Korhonen, A. "Statistical Metaphor Processing." *Computational Linguistics* 39 2013

Sporleder, C. and Li, L. "Contextual idiom detection without labelled data." Koehn, P. and Mihalcea, R. (eds.) *Proceedings of EMNLP-09* 315-323 Association for Computational Linguistics Stroudsburg, PA 2009

Steen, G., Dorst, A., Herrmann, J., Kaal, A., and Krennmayr, T. "Metaphor in usage." *Cognitive Linguistics* 21(4): 765-796 2010

Sun, L. and Korhonen, A. "Improving verb clustering with automatically acquired selectional preferences." Koehn, P. and Mihalcea, R. (eds.) *Proceedings of EMNLP-2009* 638–647 Association for Computational Linguistics Stroudsburg, PA 2009

Sun, L., Korhonen, A., and Krymolowski, Y. "Verb Class Discovery from Rich Syntactic Data." Gelbukh, A. (ed) *Proceedings of CICLING-2008, LNCS, vol. 4919* 16-27 Springer Heidelberg 2008

Turney, P. and Littman, M. "Measuring praise and criticism: Inference of semantic orientation from association." *ACM Transactions on Information Systems* 21(4): 315–346 2003

Turney, P., Neuman, Y, Assaf, D., and Cohen, Y. "Literal and Metaphorical Sense Identification through Concrete and Abstract Context." Barzilay, R. and Johnson, M. (eds.) *Proceedings of EMNLP-2011* 680–690 Association for Computational Linguistics Stroudsburg, PA 2011

Witten, I. and Frank, E. *Data Mining: Practical Machine Learning Tools and Techniques with Java Implementations* Morgan Kaufmann San Francisco 2005

Argumentation-Relevant Metaphors in Test-Taker Essays

Beata Beigman Klebanov and Michael Flor
Educational Testing Service
{bbeigmanklebanov,mflor}@ets.org

Abstract

This article discusses metaphor annotation in a corpus of argumentative essays written by test-takers during a standardized examination for graduate school admission. The quality of argumentation being the focus of the project, we developed a metaphor annotation protocol that targets metaphors that are relevant for the writer's arguments. The reliability of the protocol is κ=0.58, on a set of 116 essays (the total of about 30K content-word tokens). We found a moderate-to-strong correlation (r=0.51-0.57) between the percentage of metaphorically used words in an essay and the writing quality score. We also describe encouraging findings regarding the potential of metaphor identification to contribute to automated scoring of essays.

1 Introduction

The goal of our project is to automatically score the quality of argumentation in essays written for a standardized graduate school admission exam. Metaphors being important argumentative devices, we report on annotating data for potential training and testing of metaphor detection software that would eventually be used for automated scoring of essays.

Metaphors of various kinds can be relevant to argumentation. Some metaphors create vivid images and function as examples or as organizing ideas behind a series of examples. These are akin to pictures that are worth a thousand words, and are highly potent rhetorical devices. Metaphors of a less artistic crafting – more conventionalized ones, metaphors that we "live by" according to Lakoff and Johnson's (1980) famous tenet – subtly organize our thinking and language production in culturally coherent ways.

For an example of a vivid metaphor that helps organize the essay, consider an essay on the relationship between arts and government funding thereof (see example 1). The author's image of a piece of art as a slippery object that escapes its captor's grip as a parallel to the relationship between an artist and his or her patron/financier is a powerful image that provides a framework for the author's examples (in the preceding paragraph, Chaucer is discussed as a clever and subversive writer for his patron) and elaborations (means of "slippage", like *veiled imagery*, *multiple meanings*, etc).

(1) Great artistic productions, thus, tend to rise above the money that bought them, to bite, as it were, the hand that fed them. This is not always so, of course. But the point is that **great art is too slippery to be held in the grip of a governing power**. Through veiled imagery, multiple meanings, and carefully guarded language, a poem can both powerfully criticize a ruler and not blow its cover.

For an example of a conventional metaphor, consider the metaphor of construction/building. The connotation of *foundations* is something essential, old, solid, and lying deep, something that, once laid, remains available for new construction for a long period of time. It is often used to explain emergence of things – the existence of *foundations* (or support, or basis) is contrasted with the (presumed) idea of appearance out of nothing. Certain topics of discussion are particularly amenable for arguments from construction-upon-foundation. For example, consider an essay question "Originality does not mean thinking something that was never thought before; it means putting old ideas together in new ways," where an explanation of the emergence of something is required. Examples 2-6 show excerpts from essays answering this prompt that employ the foundation metaphor.

(2) The foundation of the United States was also based on a series of older ideas into which the fathers of our nation breathed new life.

(3) History is a progressive passing on of ideas, a process of building on the foundations laid by the previous generations. New ideas cannot stand if they are without support from the past.

(4) New discoveries and ideas are also original for some time, but eventually they become the older, accepted pieces that are the building blocks for originality.

(5) Original thinking can include old ideas which almost always are a basis for continued thought leading to new ideas.

(6) Humans are born of their ancestors, thrive from their intelligence, and are free to build on the intellectual foundations laid.

The two types of metaphors exemplified above have different argumentative roles. The first organizes a segment of an essay around it, firstly by imposing itself on the reader's mind (a property rhetoricians call *presence* (Perelman and Olbrechts-Tyteca, 1969; Gross and Dearin, 2003; Atkinson et al., 2008)), secondly by helping select supporting ideas or examples that are congruent with the parts of the target domain that are highlighted by the metaphor (this property is termed *framing* (Lakoff, 1991; Entman, 2003)), such as the idea of evasiveness purported by the ART AS A SLIPPERY OBJECT metaphor that is taken up both in the preceding Chaucer example and in an elaboration.

By contrast, metaphors "we live by" without even noticing, such as TIME IS MONEY or IDEAS ARE BUILDINGS, are not usually accorded much reader attention; they are processed by using the conventional connotation of the word as if it were an additional sense of that word, without invoking a comparison between two domains (for processing by categorization see (Bowdle and Gentner, 2005; Glucksbeg and Haught, 2006)). Thus, the word *foundation* is unlikely to elicit an image of a construction site, but rather will directly invoke the concept of something essential and primary. It is unclear to what extent such highly conventionalized metaphors that are not deliberately construed as metaphors have the framing property beyond framing induced by any lexical choice – that of stressing the chosen over the un-chosen alternative (Billig, 1996). Therefore, the fact that an essay writer used a conventional metaphor is not in itself a mark of rhetorical sophistication; it is possible, however, that, if certain metaphorical source domains are particularly apt for the given target domain (as the domain of construction to discuss emergence), using the metaphor is akin to choosing a solid though not particularly original argument.

Our interest being in metaphors that play a role in argumentation, we attempted to devise an annotation protocol that would be specifically geared towards identification of such metaphors. In what follows, we review the literature on approaches to annotating metaphors in a given discourse (section 2), we describe the protocol and the annotation procedure (section 3), report inter-annotator agreement (section 4), quantify the relationship between metaphorical density (percentage of metaphorically used words in an essay) and essay quality as measured by essay score, as well as estimate the potential usefulness of metaphor detection for automated scoring of essays (section 5.2).

2 Related Work

Much of the contemporary work on metaphor in psychological and computational veins is inspired by Lakoff and Johnson's (1980) research on conceptual metaphor. Early work in this tradition concentrated on mapping the various conceptual metaphors in use in a particular culture (Lakoff and Johnson,

1980; Lakoff and Kövecses, 1987; Kövecses, 2002). Examples for various conceptual mappings are collected, resulting in the Master Metaphor List (Lakoff et al., 1991), showing common metaphorical mappings and their instances of use. For example, the LIFE IS A JOURNEY conceptual metaphor that maps the source domain of JOURNEY to the target domain of LIFE is used in expressions such as:

- He just sails through life.
- He is headed for great things.
- If this doesn't work, I'll just try a different route.
- She'll cross that bridge when she comes to it.
- We've come a long way.

While exemplifying the extent of metaphoricity of everyday English, such a list is not directly applicable to annotating metaphors in discourse, due to the limited coverage of the expressions pertaining to each conceptual metaphor, as well as of the conceptual metaphors themselves.

Studies of discourse metaphor conducted in the Critical Discourse Analysis tradition (Musolff, 2000; Charteris-Black, 2005) analyze a particular discourse for its employment of metaphors. For example, an extensive database of metaphors in British and German newspaper discourse on European integration in the 1990s was compiled by Musolff (2000); the author did not make it clear how materials for annotation were selected.

A systematic but not comprehensive approach to creating a metaphor-rich dataset is to pre-select materials using linguistic clues (Goatly, 1997) for the presence of metaphor, such as *utterly* or *so to speak*. Shutova and Teufel (2010) report precision statistics for using different clues to detect metaphoric sentences; expressions such as *literally*, *utterly*, and *completely* indicate a metaphorical context in more than 25% of cases of their use in the British National Corpus. Such cues can aid in pre-selecting data for annotation so as to increase the proportion of materials with metaphors beyond a random sample.

Another approach is to decide on the source domains of interest in advance, use a dictionary or thesaurus to detect words belonging to the domain, and annotate them for metaphoricity (Stefanowitsch, 2006; Martin, 2006; Gedigan et al., 2006). Gedigan et al. (2006) found that more than 90% of verbs belonging to MOTION and CURE domains in a Wall Street Journal corpus were used metaphorically. Fixing the source domain is potentially appropriate if common metaphorically used domains in a given discourse have already been identified, as in (Koller et al., 2008; Beigman Klebanov et al., 2008).

A complementary approach is to fix the target domain, and do metaphor "harvesting" in a window around words belonging to the target domain. For example, Reining and Löneker-Rodman (2007) chose the lemma *Europe* to represent the target domain in the discourse on European integration. They extracted small windows around each occurrence of *Europe* in the corpus, and manually annotated them for metaphoricity. This is potentially applicable to analyzing essays, because the main target domain of the discourse is usually given in the prompt, such as *art*, *originality*. The strength of this method is its ability to focus on metaphors with argumentative potential, because the target domain, which is the topic of the essay, is directly involved. The weakness is the possibility of missing metaphors because they are not immediately adjacent to a string from the target domain.

The Metaphor Identification Procedure (MIP) is a protocol for exhaustive metaphoricity annotation proposed by the Pragglejaz group (Pragglejaz, 2007). The annotator classifies every word in a document (including prepositions) as metaphorical if it has "a more basic contemporary meaning" in other contexts than the one it has in the current context. Basic meanings are explained to be "more concrete, related to bodily action, more precise, and historically older." The authors – all highly qualified linguists who have a long history of research collaboration on the subject of metaphor – attained a kappa of 0.72 for 6 annotators for one text of 668 words and 0.62 for another text of 676 words. Shutova and Teufel (2010) used the protocol to annotate content verbs only, yielding kappa of 0.64 for 3 volunteer annotators with some linguistic background, on a set of sentences containing 142 verbs sampled from the British National Corpus. It is an open question how well educated lay people can agree on an exhaustive metaphor annotation of a text.

We note that the procedure is geared towards conceptual metaphors at large, not necessarily argumentative ones, in that the protocol does not consider the writer's purpose in using the metaphor. For example, the noun *forms* in "All one needs to use high-speed forms of communication is a computer or television and an internet cable" is a metaphor according to the MIP procedure, because the basic meaning "a shape of something" is more concrete/physical than the contextual meaning "a type of something," so a physical categorization by shape stands for a more abstract categorization into types. This metaphor could have an argumentative purport; for instance, if the types in question were actually very blurred and difficult to tell apart, by calling them forms (and, by implications, shapes), they are framed as being more clearly and easily separable than they actually are. However, since the ease of categorization of high-speed electronic communication into types is not part of the author's argument, the argumentative relevance of this metaphor is doubtful.

3 Annotation Protocol

In the present study, annotators were given the following guidelines:

> Generally speaking, a metaphor is a linguistic expression whereby something is compared to something else that it is clearly literally not, in order to make a point. Thus, in Tony Blair's famous "I haven't got a reverse gear," Tony Blair is compared to a car in order to stress his unwillingness/inability to retract his statements or actions. We would say in this case that a metaphor from a vehicle domain is used.
> ... [more examples] ...
> The first task in our study of metaphor in essays is to read essays and underline words you think are used metaphorically. Think about the point that is being made by the metaphor, and write it down. Note that a metaphor might be expressed by the author or attributed to someone else. Note also that the same metaphor can be taken up in multiple places in a text.

During training, two annotators were instructed to apply the guidelines to 6 top-scoring essays answering a prompt about the role of art in society. After they finished, sessions were held where the annotators and one of the authors of this paper discussed the annotations, including explication of the role played by the metaphor in the essay. A summary document that presents a detailed consensus annotation of 3 of the essays was circulated to the annotators. An example of an annotation is shown below (metaphors are boldfaced in the text and explained underneath):

> F. Scott Fitzgerald wrote, "There is a **dark night** in every man's soul where it is always **2 o'clock in the morning**." His words are a profound statement of human nature. Within society, we operate under a variety of social **disguises**. Some of these **masks** become so second nature that we find ourselves unable to **take** them **off**.
> (1) Dark night, 2 o'clock in the morning: True emotions are not accessible (at 2 o'clock a person is usually asleep and unaware of what is going on) and frightening to handle on one's own (scary to walk at night alone); people need mediation to help accessibility, and also company to alleviate the fear. Art provides both. This metaphor puts forward the two main arguments: accessibility and sharing.
> (2) Masks, take off, disguises: could be referring to the domain of theater/performance. Makes the point that what people do in real life to themselves is superficially similar to what art (theater) does to performers – hiding their true identity. In the theater, the hiding is temporary and completely reversible at will, there is really no such thing as inability to take off the mask. The socially-inflicted hiding is not necessarily under the person's control, differently from a theatrical mask. Supports and extends the accessibility argument: not just lack of courage or will, but lack of control to access the true selves.

The actual annotation then commenced, on a sample of essays answering a different question (the data will be described in section 3.1). Annotators were instructed to mark metaphors in the text using a graphical interface that was specially developed for the project. The guidelines for the actual annotation are shown below:

> During training, you practiced careful reading while paying attention to non-literal language and saw how metaphors work in their context. At the annotation stage, you are not asked to explicitly interpret the metaphor and identify its argumentative contribution (or rather, its attempted argumentative contribution), only to mark metaphors, trusting your intuition that you *could* try to interpret the metaphor in context if needed.

Note that we have not provided formal definitions of what a literal sense is in order to not interfere with intuitive judgments of metaphoricity (differently from Pragglejaz (2007), for example, who provide definition of a basic sense). Neither have we set up an explicit classification task, whereby annotators are required to classify every single word in the text as a metaphor or a non-metaphor (again, differently from Pragglejaz (2007)); in our task, annotators were instructed to mark metaphors while they read. This is in the spirit of Steen's (2008) notion of deliberate metaphors – words and phrases that the writer actually meant to produce as a metaphor, as opposed to cases where the writer did not have a choice, such as using *in* for an expression like *in time*, due to the pervasiveness of the time-as-space metaphor. Note, however, that Steen's notion is writer-based; since we have no access to the writers of the essays, we side with an educated lay reader and his or her perception of a metaphorical use.

The annotators were instructed to give the author the benefit of the doubt and *not* to assume that a common metaphor is necessarily unintenional:

> When deciding whether to attribute to the author the intention of making a point using a metaphor, please be as liberal as you can and give the author the benefit of the doubt. Specifically, if something is a rather common metaphor that still happens to fit nicely into the argument the author is making, we assume that the author intended it that way.

To clarify what kinds of metaphors are excluded by our guidelines, we explained as follows:

> In contrast, consider cases where an expression might be perhaps formally classified as a metaphor, but the literal sense cannot be seen as relevant to the author's argument. For example, consider the following sentence from Essay 2 from our training material: "Seeing the beauty of nature or hearing a moving piece of music may drive one to perhaps try to replicate that beauty *in* a style of one's own." Look at the italicized word – the preposition *in*. According to some theories of metaphor, that would constitute a metaphorical use: Literally, *in* means inside some container; since style is not literally a container, the use of *in* here is non-literal. Suppose now that the non-literal interpretation invites the reader to see style as a container. A container might have more or less room, can be full or empty, can be rigid or flexible, can contain items of the same or different sorts – these are some potential images that go with viewing something as a container, yet none of them seems to be relevant to whatever the author is saying about style, that is, that it is unique (one's own) and yet the result is not quite original (replication).

The two annotators who participated in the task hold BA degrees in Linguistics, but have no background in metaphor theory. They were surprised and bemused by an example like *in style*, commenting that it would never have occurred to them to mark it as a metaphor. In general, the thrust of this protocol is to identify metaphorical expressions that are noticeable and support the author's argumentative moves; yet, we targeted a reasonable timeline for completing the task, with about 30 minutes per text, therefore we did not require a detailed analysis of the marked metaphors as done during training.

3.1 Data

Annotation was performed on 116 essays written on the following topic: "High-speed electronic communications media, such as electronic mail and television, tend to prevent meaningful and thoughtful communication." Test-takers are instructed to present their perspective on the issue, using relevant reasons and/or examples to support their views. Test-takers are given 45 minutes to compose an essay. The essays were sampled from the dataset analyzed in Attali et al. (2013), with oversampling of longer essays. In the Attali et al. (2013) study, each essay was scored for the overall quality of English argumentative composition; thus, to receive the maximum score, an essay should present a cogent, well-articulated analysis of the complexities of the issue and convey meaning skillfully. Each essay was scored by 16 professional raters on a scale of 1 to 6, allowing plus and minus scores as well, quantified as 0.33 – thus, a score of 4- is rendered as 3.67. This fine-grained scale resulted in a high mean pairwise inter-rater correlation (r=0.79). We use the average of 16 raters as the final score for each essay. This dataset provides a fine-grained ranking of the essays, with almost no two essays getting exactly the same score.

For the 116 essays, the mean length was 478 words (min: 159, max: 793, std: 142); mean score: 3.82 (min: 1.81, max: 5.77, std: 0.73). Table 1 shows the distribution of essay scores.

Score	Number of Essays	Proportion of Essays
2	4	0.034
3	33	0.284
4	59	0.509
5	19	0.164
6	1	0.009

Table 1: Score distribution in the essay data. The first column shows the rounded score. For the sake of presentation in this table, all scores were rounded to integer scores, so a score of 3.33 was counted as 3, and a score of 3.5 was counted as 4.

4 Inter-Annotator Agreement and Parts of Speech

The inter-annotator agreement on the total of 55,473 word tokens was κ=0.575. In this section, we investigate the relationship between part of speech and metaphor use, as well as part of speech and inter-annotator agreement.

For this discussion, words that appear in the prompt (essay topic) are excluded from all sets. Furthermore, we concentrate on content words only (as identified by the OpenNLP tagger[1]). Table 2 shows the split of the content-word annotations by part of speech, as well as the reliability figures. We report information for each of the two annotators separately, as well as for the union of their annotations. We report the union as we hypothesize that a substantial proportion of apparent disagreements between annotators are attention slips rather than substantive disagreements; this phenomenon was attested in a previous study (Beigman Klebanov et al., 2008).

POS	Count	A1	A2	A1⋃A2	κ
All	55,473	2,802	2,591	3,788	0.575
Cont.	29,207	2,380	2,251	3,211	0.580
Noun	12,119	1,033	869	1,305	0.596
Adj	4,181	253	239	356	0.525
Verb	9,561	1,007	1,039	1,422	0.563
Adv	3,346	87	104	128	0.650

Table 2: Reliability by part of speech. The column Count shows the total number of words in the given part of speech across the 116 essays. Columns A1 and A2 show the number of items marked as metaphors by annotators 1 and 2, respectively, while Column A1⋃A2 shows numbers of items in the union of the two annotations. The second row presents the overall figure for content words.

Nouns constitute 41.5% of all content words; they are 43.4% of all content-word metaphors for annotator 1, 38.6% for annotator 2, and 40.6% for the union of the two annotations. Nouns are therefore represented in the metaphor annotated data in their general distribution proportions. Of all nouns, 7%-8.5% are identified as metaphors by a single annotator, while 10.8% of the nouns are metaphors in the union annotation.

[1] http://opennlp.apache.org/index.html

Verbs are 32.7% of all content words; they are 42.3% of all content-word metaphors for annotator 1, 46.2% for annotator 2, and 44.3% in the union. Verbs are therefore over-represented in the metaphor annotated data relative to their general distribution proportions. Of all verbs, 10.5%-10.9% are identified as metaphors by a single annotator, while 14.9% are metaphors in the union annotation.

Adjectives are 14.3% of all content words; they are 10.6% of all content-word metaphors for annotator 1, 10.6% for annotator 2, and 11.1% in the union. Adjectives are therefore somewhat under-represented in the metaphor annotated data with respect to their general distribution. About 6% of adjectives are identified as metaphors in individual annotations, and 8.5% in the union annotation.

Adverbs are 11.5% of all content words; they are 3.7% of all content-word metaphors for annotator 1 and 4.6% for annotator 2, and 4% in the union. Adverbs are heavily under-represented in the metaphor annotated data with respect to their general distribution. Of all non-prompt adverbs, about 3-4% are identified as metaphors.

The data clearly points towards the propensity of verbs towards metaphoricity, relative to words from other parts of speech. This is in line with reports in the literature that identify verbs as central carriers of metaphorical vehicles: Cameron (2003) found that about 50% of metaphors in educational discourse are realized by verbs, beyond their distributional proportion; this finding prompted Shutova et al. (2013) to concentrate exclusively on verbs.

According to Goatly (1997), parts of speech differ in the kinds of metaphors they realize in terms of the recognizability of the metaphorical use as such. Nouns are more recognizable as metaphors than other word classes for the following two reasons: (1) Since nouns are referring expressions, they reveal very strongly the clashes between conventional and unconventional reference; (2) Since nouns often refer to vivid, imaginable entities, they are more easliy recognized than metaphors of other parts of speech. Moreover, morphological derivation away from nouns – for example, by affixation – leads to more lexicalized and less noticeable metaphors than the original nouns.

Goatly's predictions seem to be reflected in inter-annotator agreement figures for nouns versus adjectives and verbs, with nouns yielding higher reliability of identification than verbs and adjectives, with the latter two categories having more cases where only one but not both of the annotators noticed a metaphorical use. Since adverbs are the most distant from nouns in terms of processes of morphological derivation, one would expect them to be less easily noticeable, yet in our annotation adverbs are the most reliably classified category.

Inspecting the metaphorically used adverbs, we find that a small number of adverbs cover the bulk of the volume: *together* (11), *closer* (11), *away* (10), *back* (8) account for 46% of the adverbs marked by annotator 1 in our dataset. Almost all cases of *together* come from a use in the phrasal verb *bring together* (8 cases), in expressions like "bringing the world together into one cyberspace without borders" or "electronic mail could bring people closer together" or "bringing society together." In fact, 6 of the 11 cases of *closer* are part of the construction *bring closer together*, and the other cases have similar uses like "our conversations are more meaningful because we are closer through the internet."

Interestingly, the metaphorical uses of *away* also come from phrasal constructions that are used for arguing precisely the opposite point – that cyber-communications drive people away from each other: "email, instant messaging, and television support a shift away from throughful communication," "mass media and communications drive people away from one another," "by typing a message ... you can easily get away from the conversation."

It seems that the adverbs marked for metaphoricity in our data tend to be (a) part of phrasal constructions, and (b) part of a commonly made argument for or against electronic communication – that it (metaphorically) brings people together, or (metaphorically) drives them apart by making the actual togetherness (co-location) unnecessary for communication. The adverbs are therefore not of the derivationally complex kind Goatly has in mind, and their noticeability might be enhanced by being part of a common argumentative move in the examined materials, especially since the annotators were instructed to look out for metaphors that support the writer's argument.

5 Metaphor and Content Scoring

In order to assess the potential of metaphor detection to contribute to essay scoring, we performed two tests: correlation with essay scores and a regression analysis in order to check whether metaphor use contributes information that is beyond what is captured by a state-of-art essay scoring system.

As a metaphor-derived feature, we calculated **metaphorical density**, that is, the percentage of metaphorically used words in an essay: All words marked as metaphors in an essay were counted (content or other), and the total was divided by essay length.

5.1 E-rater

As a reference system, we use e-rater (Attali and Burstein, 2006), a state-of-art essay scoring system developed at Educational Testing Service.[2] E-rater computes more than 100 micro-features, which are aggregated into macro-features aligned with specific aspects of the writing construct. The system incorporates macro-features measuring grammar, usage, mechanics, style, organization and development, lexical complexity, and vocabulary usage. Table 3 gives examples of micro-features covered by the different macro-features.

Macro-Feature	Example Micro-Features
Grammar, Usage, and Mechanics	agreement errors verb formation errors missing punctuation
Style	passive, very long or very short sentences, excessive repetition
Organization and Development	use of discourse elements: thesis, support, conclusion
Lexical Complexity	average word frequency average word length
Vocabulary	similarity to vocabulary in high- vs low-scoring essays

Table 3: Features used in e-rater (Attali and Burstein, 2006).

E-rater models are built using linear regression on large samples of test-taker essays. We use an e-rater model built at Educational Testing Service using a large number of essays across different prompts, with no connection to the current project and its authors. This model obtains Pearson correlations of r=0.935 with the human scores. The excellent performance of the system leaves little room for improvement; yet, none of the features in e-rater specifically targets the use of figurative language, so it is interesting to see the extent to which metaphor use could help explain additional variance.

[2]http://www.ets.org/erater/about/

5.2 Results

We found that metaphorical density attains correlation of r=0.507 with essay score using annotations of annotator 1, r=0.556 for annotator 2, and r=0.570 using the union of the two annotators. It is clearly the case that better essays tend to have higher proportions of metaphors.

We ran a regression analysis with essay score as the dependent variable and e-rater raw score and metaphor density in the union annotation as two independent variables. The correlation with essay score improved from 0.935 using e-rater alone to 0.937 using the regression equation (the adjusted R^2 of the model improved from 0.874 to 0.876). While the contribution of metaphor feature is not statistically significant for the size of our dataset (n=116, p=0.07), we are cautiously optimistic that metaphor detection can make a contribution to essay scoring when the process is automated and a larger-scale evaluation can be performed.

6 Conclusion

This article discusses annotation of metaphors in a corpus of argumentative essays written by test-takers during a standardized examination for graduate school admission. The quality of argumentation being the focus of the project, we developed a metaphor annotation protocol that targets metaphors that are relevant for the writer's arguments. The reliability of the protocol is κ=0.58, on a set of 116 essays (a total of about 30K content word tokens).

We found a moderate-to-strong correlation (r=0.51-0.57) between the density of metaphors in an essay (percentage of metaphorically used words) and the writing quality score as provided by professional essay raters.

As the annotation protocol is operationally efficient (30 minutes per essay of about 500 words), moderately reliable (κ=0.58), and uses annotators that do not possess specialized knowledge and training in metaphor theory, we believe it is feasible to annotate a large set of essays for the purpose of building a supervised machine learning system for detection of metaphors in test-taker essays. The observed correlations of metaphor use with essay score, as well as the fact that metaphor use is not captured by state-of-art essay scoring systems, point towards the potential usefulness of a metaphor detection system for essay scoring.

References

Nathan Atkinson, David Kaufer, and Suguru Ishizaki. 2008. Presence and Global Presence in Genres of Self-Presentation: A Framework for Comparative Analysis. *Rhetoric Society Quarterly*, 38(3):1–27.

Yigal Attali and Jill Burstein. 2006. Automated Essay Scoring With e-rater®V.2. *Journal of Technology, Learning, and Assessment*, 4(3).

Yigal Attali, Will Lewis, and Michael Steier. 2013. Scoring with the computer: Alternative procedures for improving reliability of holistic essay scoring. *Language Testing*, 30(1):125–141.

Beata Beigman Klebanov, Eyal Beigman, and Daniel Diermeier. 2008. Analyzing disagreements. In *COLING 2008 workshop on Human Judgments in Computational Linguistics*, pages 2–7, Manchester, UK.

Michael Billig. 1996. *Arguing and Thinking: A Rhetorical Approach to Social Psychology*. Cambridge University Press, Cambridge.

Brian Bowdle and Dedre Gentner. 2005. The career of metaphor. *Psychological Review*, 112(1):193–216.

Lynne Cameron. 2003. *Metaphor in Educational Discourse*. Continuum, London.

Jonathan Charteris-Black. 2005. *Politicians and rhetoric: The persuasive power of metaphors*. Palgrave MacMillan, Houndmills, UK and New York.

Robert Entman. 2003. Cascading activation: Contesting the white houses frame after 9/11. *Political Communication*, 20:415–432.

Matt Gedigan, John Bryant, Srini Narayanan, and Branimir Ciric. 2006. Catching metaphors. In *PProceedings of the 3rd Workshop on Scalable Natural Language Understanding*, pages 41–48, New York.

Sam Glucksbeg and Catrinel Haught. 2006. On the relation between metaphor and simile: When comparison fails. *Mind and Language*, 21(3):360–378.

Andrew Goatly. 1997. *The Language of Metaphors*. Routledge, London.

Alan Gross and Ray Dearin. 2003. *Chaim Perelman*. Albany: SUNY Press.

Zoltan Kövecses. 2002. *Metaphor: A Practical Introduction*. Oxford University Press.

Veronika Koller, Andrew Hardie, Paul Rayson, and Elena Semino. 2008. Using a semantic annotation tool for the analysis of metaphor in discourse. *Metaphorik.de*, 15:141–160.

George Lakoff and Mark Johnson. 1980. *Metaphors we live by*. University of Chicago Press, Chicago.

George Lakoff and Zoltan Kövecses. 1987. Metaphors of anger in japanese. In D. Holland and N. Quinn, editors, *Cultural Models in Language and Thought*. Cambridge: Cambridge University Press.

George Lakoff, Jane Espenson, Adele Goldberg, and Alan Schwartz. 1991. Master Metaphor List, Second Draft Copy. Cognitive Linguisics Group, Univeristy of California, Berkeley: http://araw.mede.uic.edu/~alansz/metaphor/METAPHORLIST.pdf.

George Lakoff. 1991. Metaphor and war: The metaphor system used to justify war in the gulf. *Peace Research*, 23:25–32.

James Martin. 2006. A corpus-based analysis of context effects on metaphor comprehension. In Anatol Stefanowitsch and Stefan Gries, editors, *Corpus-Based Approaches to Metaphor and Metonymy*. Berlin: Mouton de Gruyter.

Andreas Musolff. 2000. *Mirror images of Europe: Metaphors in the public debate about Europe in Britain and Germany*. München: Iudicium. Annotated data is available at http://www.dur.ac.uk/andreas.musolff/Arcindex.htm.

Chaïm Perelman and Lucie Olbrechts-Tyteca. 1969. *The New Rhetoric: A Treatise on Argumentation*. Notre Dame, Indiana: University of Notre Dame Press. Translated by John Wilkinson and Purcell Weaver from French original published in 1958.

Group Pragglejaz. 2007. MIP: A Method for Identifying Metaphorically Used Words in Discourse. *Metaphor and Symbol*, 22(1):1–39.

Astrid Reining and Birte Löneker-Rodman. 2007. Corpus-driven metaphor harvesting. In *Proceedings of the Workshop on Computational Approaches to Figurative Language*, pages 5–12, Rochester, New York.

Ekaterina Shutova and Simone Teufel. 2010. Metaphor Corpus Annotated for Source-Target Domain Mappings. In *Proceedings of LREC*, Valetta, Malta.

Ekaterina Shutova, Simone Teufel, and Anna Korhonen. 2013. Statistical metaphor processing. *Computational Linguistics*, 39(1).

Gerard Steen. 2008. The Paradox of Metaphor: Why We Need a Three-Dimensional Model of Metaphor. *Metaphor and Symbol*, 23(4):213–241.

Anatol Stefanowitsch. 2006. Corpus-based approaches to metaphor and metonymy. In Anatol Stefanowitsch and Stefan Gries, editors, *Corpus-Based Approaches to Metaphor and Metonymy*. Berlin: Mouton de Gruyter.

Relational words have high metaphoric potential

Anja Jamrozik
Northwestern University
Department of Psychology - 2029 Sheridan Road
Evanston, IL 60208-2710, USA
a.jamrozik@u.northwestern.edu

Eyal Sagi
Northwestern University
Kellogg School - 2001 Sheridan Road
Evanston, IL 60208-2710, USA
eyal@u.northwestern.edu

Micah Goldwater
Northwestern University
Department of Psychology - 2029 Sheridan Road
Evanston, IL 60208-2710, USA
micahbg@gmail.com

Dedre Gentner
Northwestern University
Department of Psychology - 2029 Sheridan Road
Evanston, IL 60208-2710, USA
gentner@northwestern.edu

Abstract

What influences the likelihood that a word will be used metaphorically? We tested whether the likelihood of metaphorical use is related to the relationality of a word's meaning. Relational words name relations between entities. We predicted that relational words, such as verbs (e.g., *speak*) and relational nouns (e.g., *marriage*) would be more likely to be used metaphorically than words that name entities (e.g., *item*). In two experiments, we collected expert ratings of metaphoricity for uses of verbs, relational nouns, and entity nouns collected from a corpus search. As predicted, uses of relational words were rated as more metaphorical than uses of entity words. We discuss how these findings could inform NLP models of metaphor.

1 Introduction

Our goal is to assess the *metaphoric potential* of words and word classes—by which we mean the likelihood that the word (or word class) will be used metaphorically. By *metaphorical use*, we mean the use of a word to convey ideas that are not part of its basic or standard meaning. We note that metaphoric potential does not equate to metaphoric salience. Many common metaphorical uses are not particularly salient. These include non-spatial, abstract uses of prepositions (e.g., *in* love, *between* assignments) and metaphorical uses of verbs (e.g., *run* for office, *fall* behind).

One could question whether it is useful to identify the kind of metaphorical uses just mentioned. Shutova, Tuefel, & Korhonen (2012) point out that it may not be relevant to NLP applications to identify highly conventionalized or "dead" metaphorical uses, ones for which a metaphorical sense has become dominant and earlier literal senses have become obsolete. An example is the verb *impress,* which was originally used in printing contexts and meant 'to make a mark with pressure' but now is typically used to mean 'to produce admiration in someone'. While we agree that identifying such 'dead' metaphors may not be useful, we note that there are many conventional metaphors that also retain a healthy literal sense; and in these cases, identifying their metaphorical uses can be challenging. An example is the word *glow,* which can be used literally (The lamp *glows* dimly) as well as metaphorically (Her face *glows* with joy). In our research, we will consider both conventional and novel extensions of a word's meaning but will focus more on conventional metaphorical uses.

Many factors influence a word's metaphoric potential—including its conventionality as a prior metaphoric source, its familiarity, and whether it belongs to a conceptual system whose other members are often used metaphorically[1]. We focus here on a relatively unexplored factor: namely, the relationality of the word's meaning.

Relational words are words that take more than one argument. These include verbs (KNOW(Sue, Ida)), prepositions (ON(fence, hill)), and relational

[1] For example, one might be able to say "Let me slide this to him" meaning "Let me communicate this to him in a smooth manner)," because the "conduit" metaphoric system (Reddy, 1979; Lakoff & Johnson, 1980) includes other instances of caused-physical-motion verbs used to convey communication of ideas (e.g., "Is this message getting across to you?").

nouns[2] (FRIEND OF(John, George). Relational nouns (e.g., *guest, host, party*). which name relations or systems of relations, can be contrasted with entity nouns (e.g., *zebra, thing*), which name entities defined by their intrinsic properties (see Gentner & Kurtz, 2005; Goldwater Markman & Stilwell, 2011, and Markman & Stilwell, 2001).

Goldwater and Willits (2010) explored ways to distinguish relational from entity nouns based on their distributional patterns. All of the nouns from the Goldwater et al. (2011), Gentner & Kurtz (2005) and Gentner & Asmuth (2008) studies were normed for their relationality by naïve participants, who rated to what degree each word expressed relational or entity meanings. Goldwater and Willits analyzed the distributions of the top 50 highest rated relational nouns and top 25 entity nouns on a 10,000 word corpus from Wikipedia.com. The two kinds of nouns were found to have distinct distributional patterns. For relational nouns, the most frequent immediate following word is a preposition connecting the noun to another term (as in 'proportion *of* X' or 'barrier *to* X')[3]. In contrast, the most frequent immediate follower for entity nouns is *and*[4]. These distributional patterns can be used to predict noun type. Given two words, their distributional similarity can predict whether they are of the same noun type or different noun type with close to 90% accuracy. Although further study is needed of how well these results extend to a larger sample of nouns, we believe this is a promising direction.

Our hypothesis that metaphorical potential is related to relationality is supported by evidence that relational words are more *mutable* than entity words—that is, the meanings of relational words adjust more to fit their contexts than do the meanings of entity nouns (Gentner, 1981). Psycholinguistic studies of sentence interpretation have found this pattern both across word classes (nouns vs. verbs) and within the noun class (entity nouns vs. relational nouns). For example, when participants were asked to paraphrase semantically strained sentences in which the noun did not meet the argument specification of the verb (e.g., The car laughed), their paraphrases were far more likely to preserve the meanings of the nouns than of the verbs (Gentner & France, 1988) (e.g., 'The automobile sputtered and refused to start'). Further evidence comes from studies testing recognition memory of nouns and verbs (Kersten & Earles, 2004). Verbs were recognized better if found in the same context as at encoding, but nouns were recognized equally well whether in the same context or in a new context. Kersten and Earles suggested that this difference stemmed from the greater mutability of verbs (Gentner, 1981). Because the meanings of verbs adjust more to their contexts than do the meanings of nouns, a verb may be interpreted as having very different meanings at encoding and at test. This made it difficult for participants to recognize that the same word was used in both cases.

There is also evidence that relational nouns have greater mutability than entity nouns. Using a similar paradigm to the one used by Kersten and Earles (2004), Asmuth and Gentner (2005) gave participants conceptual combinations consisting of one relational noun and one entity noun (e.g., *a truck limitation, a barrier peanut*) and later tested their recognition memory for the individual nouns, which were either presented in the old context (the same context as at encoding) or in a new context. Overall, recognition of entity nouns was better than recognition of relational nouns. Additionally, recognition for relational nouns was more impaired by a shift to a new context than was recognition of entity nouns. This is consistent with the mutability claim that relational nouns are encoded in a context-dependent manner.

To summarize, the evidence that relational words are more mutable than entity words suggest that they should have greater metaphoric potential. If a word's meaning readily adjusts to its context, this can result in metaphoric extensions that go beyond the word's basic or standard meaning. Since relational words are more mutable than entity words, they should be more likely to be extended in this way.

We test this prediction both across and within word classes. Comparing across word classes, we predict that verbs will have greater metaphoric potential than nouns. Comparing within word class,

---

[2] A common test for relational nouns involves the use of genitive *of* (Barker and Dowty, 1993). For example, *friend* is a relational noun, and "friend of John" and "John's friend" are both grammatical and interchangeable. The *of* form is not grammatical for non-relational nouns (e.g., John's truck, *truck of John) (Barker, 1995).

[3] Goldwater and Willits found that relational nouns were most frequently followed by *of*, but distributional approaches could be extended to other common role-bearing terms.

we predict that relational nouns will have greater metaphoric potential than entity nouns.

There is already evidence for the predicted difference between word classes: metaphorical uses of verbs have been found to be more common than metaphorical uses of nouns in poetry (Brooke-Rose, 1958), in classroom discourse (e.g., Cameron, 2003), and across various spoken and written genres (e.g., Shutova & Teufel, 2010; Steen, Dorst, Herrmann, Kaal, Krennmayr, & Pasma, 2010).

In the studies that follow, we tested our predictions using data collected from a corpus search. We randomly sampled uses of verbs, relational nouns, and entity nouns and collected novelty and metaphoricity ratings for each of these uses. We were particularly interested in the pattern among conventional metaphorical uses, which are the most challenging to identify with NLP methods.

2 Experiment 1

2.1 Materials

The materials consisted of 20 uses each of nine entity nouns, eighteen relational nouns[5], and nine verbs. The entity and relational nouns were selected based on data from a previous rating task (the same as provided Goldwater and Willits with their sample). The entity nouns we selected were rated as conveying an entity meaning to a higher degree than the relational nouns, and vice versa, all *ps* < .001. The nine verbs were selected to match the frequencies of the nouns, using data from the Corpus of Contemporary American English (COCA) (Davies, 2008-). There were no differences in the frequencies of the word types, $F(3, 32) = .857, p = .474$.

We collected a random sample of 20 uses of each of the 36 words from COCA, with an equal number from the spoken, fiction, magazine, news, and academic registers. We used the following criteria to determine whether a word use would be included in the sample. First, the word had to be used as a noun or verb, depending on its preselected word type[6] (e.g., for the verb *talk*, we only collected uses in which *talk* was used as a verb). Second, the word had to be used in a full sentence or phrase, so as to give sufficient context to determine how metaphorical the use was. Third, the sentence had to be a statement, not a question. Finally, the word could only appear once in the sentence.

2.2 Rating Task

The three raters were Ph.D. students of English or Comparative Literature. They were chosen because they had extensive experience identifying figurative language and would be able to identify metaphors that may not have been particularly salient to average readers.

The raters were given sets of sentences with the key terms bolded and underlined: e.g.,

> The human mind, the only **device** capable of traveling through time, tends to want to stay in its own time.
>
> A smartphone or other technological **device** used during worship also can be a distraction.

They were instructed to rate the metaphoricity and the novelty of the indicated words, on two separate scales from 1 (not at all novel /metaphorical) to 6 (very novel/metaphorical). The separate ratings were used to ensure that raters were not conflating novelty and metaphoricity. For each item, we calculated the average of the individual novelty and metaphoricity scores assigned by the raters.

2.3 Results

As predicted, we found that the metaphor ratings differed across word types. We conducted an ANOVA with the average metaphor ratings for each use as the dependent variable. The type of word rated (Entity Noun, Relational Noun, or Verb) was the independent variable and the specific word was a random effect. This resulted in a marginally significant effect of word type, $F(2, 684) = 3.22, p = .053$. Post-hoc Tukey HSD tests revealed that uses of verbs ($M = 1.77, SD = 0.76$) and relational nouns ($M = 1.75, SD = 0.91$) were rated as more metaphorical than uses of entity nouns ($M = 1.27, SD = 0.61$), *ps* < .001.

The difference between word types was also

[5] There were two different kinds of relational nouns (*schema* nouns, which refer to relational systems, e.g., *party*, and *role* nouns, which refer to roles within such systems, e.g., *guest*), but we do not distinguish them in the analyses that follow.

[6] We reserve the use of the term *word class* for accepted syntactic distinctions (e.g., nouns vs. verbs) and use the term *word type* to differentiate the kinds of words compared in these experiments.

marginal when analyzing only conventional uses (i.e., those rated "1" for novelty), $F(2, 437) = 2.80$, $p = .075$. Uses of verbs ($M = 1.36$, $SD = 0.33$) and relational nouns ($M = 1.27$, $SD = 0.41$) were rated as more metaphorical than uses of entity nouns ($M = 1.16$, $SD = 0.29$), $ps < .01$. No differences in metaphoricity were observed between word types for novel uses (i.e., those rated higher than "1" for novelty), $F(2, 213) = 1.49, p = 0.24$.

While these results are only marginally significant, they provide encouragement that relationality might influence the metaphoric potential of a word.

2.4 Concreteness, imageability and metaphoric potential

One concern regarding Experiment 1 is that we did not control for concreteness or imeageability of the words. Previous research is conflicted about what effects concreteness and imageability should have on a word's metaphorical potential. On the one hand, it has been argued that greater concreteness (e.g., Katz, 1989) and imageability (e.g., Goatly, 2011) should result in greater metaphoricity. However, previous work by Gentner and Asmuth (2008) has shown that relational words, which we found to have greater metaphorical potential, tend to be less concrete and imageable than entity words. In accordance with these findings, we found that concreteness and imageability of the words (using data from MRC Psycholinguistic Database - Coltheart, 1981) varied across word types (concreteness: $F(2, 26) = 27.36$, $p < .001$; imageability: $F(2, 26) = 15.71$, $p < .001$). Entity nouns were more concrete and imageable than relational nouns and verbs, all $ps < .001$.

The entity nouns were more concrete and imageable than the relational words, but their uses were less metaphorical. Thus in our sample, the relationship between concreteness, imageability, and metaphoricity was the opposite of that predicted by Katz (1989) and Goatly (2011)[7]: more concrete words were rated as less metaphorical, $r(27) = -.43$, $p = .021$. (The relationship between imageability and metaphoricity was not significant ($r(27) = -.30, p = .117$)). Because of these findings, in the next experiment we controlled for concreteness and imageability across word classes.

[7] It is possible that Katz's and Goatly's predictions drew on different contexts of use from those in our corpus.

3 Experiment 2

3.1 Materials

The materials consisted of 20 uses each of eight entity nouns, sixteen relational nouns, and eight verbs. The words were selected in the same manner as those in Experiment 1, except that in addition to controlling for frequency across word types, we also controlled for concreteness and imageability. In the resulting sets, there were no differences in the concreteness of the word types (Coltheart, 1981), $F(2, 29) = .745, p = .484$, in the imageability of the word types (Coltheart, 1981), $F(2, 29) = .043$, $p = .958$, nor in the frequencies of the word types (using frequency data from COCA), $F(2, 29) = .144, p = .867$.

3.2 Rating task

The raters were three Ph.D. students of English or Comparative Literature who had not participated in the first experiment. The raters received the same instructions and followed the same procedure as in the first experiment.

3.3 Results

Overall, as predicted, we found that uses of relational words were rated as more metaphorical than uses of entity words. An ANOVA like that used in Experiment 1 showed that the average metaphor ratings differed across word types, $F(2, 608) = 3.77, p < .05$. Uses of verbs ($M = 2.35$, $SD = 1.69$) were rated as more metaphorical than uses of entity nouns ($M = 1.47$, $SD = 1.08$) and relational nouns ($M = 1.67$, $SD = 1.21$), $ps < .001$. However (in contrast to the first study) relational nouns were not significantly more metaphorical overall than entity nouns ($p = .17$).

The pattern was stronger when we looked only within conventional uses[8] (i.e., those rated "1" for novelty), $F(2, 513) = 4.22$, $p < .05$. Conventional uses of verbs were rated as more metaphorical ($M = 2.19$, $SD = 1.59$) than uses of entity nouns ($M = 1.16$, $SD = 0.56$) and relational nouns ($M = 1.42$, $SD = 0.96$), all $ps < .001$. Uses of relational nouns were also rated as more metaphorical than uses of entity nouns, $p < .05$.

As in the first study, there were no differences

[8] Conventional uses made up 85% (545/640) of the sample.

between word types for the novel uses (i.e., those rated higher than "1" for novelty), $F(2, 70) = 1.22$, $p = 0.31$.

4 Discussion

The results of two experiments provide support for the hypothesis that relational words have greater metaphoric potential than entity words. In the first experiment, verbs and relational nouns were rated as marginally more metaphorical than entity nouns. In the second experiment, in which concreteness and imageability were equated across the word types, verbs were rated more metaphorical than nouns. Within conventional uses, verbs were rated as more metaphorical than nouns, and relational nouns were rated more metaphorical than entity nouns.

4.1 Relationality and language change

These findings accord with our prediction that relational words have greater metaphorical potential than entity words, and that this pattern is stronger for conventional uses. Why is this the case? We conjecture that there may be two paths at work here. First, metaphor conventionalization may result in words acquiring relational senses. According to the Career of Metaphor hypothesis (Bowdle & Gentner, 1999, 2005; Gentner, Bowdle, Wolff, & Boronat, 2001; Gentner & Wolff, 1997) when a word is used in a novel metaphoric way, the use is processed by aligning the literal target and base of the metaphor in order to abstract their common structure. If the base term is repeatedly paired with other similar target terms, the structure abstracted through alignment may become another conventional meaning of the base term. Providing some initial support for this idea, Zharikov and Gentner (2002) traced the meanings of current relational words (e.g., *bridge*), and found that their relational meanings had evolved from earlier concrete, entity meanings. This idea also fits with accounts that argue that metaphoric use is one of the mechanisms precipitating semantic shifts in meaning (e.g., Traugott, 2004).

A second conjecture is that because relational words often identify deep relations among their arguments, uses of relational words across domains should result in more apt and relevant metaphors, which may therefore be more readily accepted. This means that metaphorical uses of relational words may be more likely to become conventionalized than metaphorical uses of entity words.

4.2 Applications to NLP

The metaphoric uses we found in our experiments were in general not high-salient, striking figures of speech. Moreover, these metaphoric uses coexisted with literal uses of the same word (conventional non-metaphoric language was still the most common form). It is these unstriking, conventional metaphorical uses that pose a challenge for NLP (Shutova, Tuefel, & Korhonen, 2012).

How can NLP models of metaphor utilize our results? One possibility is to use differences in metaphoric potential among word types to inform searches for metaphoric language in corpora. Such an application would naturally also require a method for identifying relational words. Of course, since verbs appear to have a higher metaphoric potential than nouns, just using grammatical category information that is already available can make a substantial gain. Moreover, the distributional findings discussed earlier offer a potential way to distinguish relational from entity nouns (Goldwater & Willits, 2010). Assuming their results generalize, it might be feasible to distinguish relational nouns from entity nouns using distributional information.

In sum, we believe that taking into account the relationality of words has the potential to improve NLP models of metaphor. We look forward to the research that would come from uniting this psychological research with current research in NLP.

Acknowledgments

The research described here was conducted in the Spatial Intelligence and Learning Center (SILC), a center funded by NSF grant SBE-0541957. We thank the six raters who participated in our rating tasks and the Cognition and Language Lab.

References

Asmuth, J. & Gentner, D. (2005). Context sensitivity of relational nouns. *Proceedings of the Twenty-seventh Annual Meeting of the Cognitive Science Society*, 163-168.

Barker, C. (1995). *Possessive Descriptions*. Stanford, CA: CSLI Publications.

Barker, C., & Dowty, D. (1993). Non-verbal thematic proto-roles. *Proceedings of the North East Linguistic Society 23*, 49-62.

Brooke-Rose, C. (1958). *A grammar of metaphor*. London: Seeker & Warburg.

Bowdle, B., & Gentner, D. (1999). Metaphor comprehension: From comparison to categorization. *Proceedings of the Twenty-First Annual Conference of the Cognitive Science Society*, 90-95.

Bowdle, B., & Gentner, D. (2005). The career of metaphor. *Psychological Review, 112*(1), 193-216.

Cameron, L. (2003). *Metaphor in educational discourse*. New York: Continuum.

Coltheart, M. (1981). The MRC Psycholinguistic Database. *Quarterly Journal of Experimental Psychology, 33A*, 497-505.

Davies, M. (2008-) The Corpus of Contemporary American English (COCA): 425 million words, 1990-present. Available online at http://corpus.byu.edu/coca/.

Gentner, D. (1981). Some interesting differences between nouns and verbs. *Cognition and Brain Theory, 4*, 161-178.

Gentner, D., & Asmuth, J. (2008). Can relationality be distinguished from abstractness in noun mutability? *Proceedings of the 30th Annual Conference of the Cognitive Science Society,* 863-868.

Gentner, D., Bowdle, B., Wolff, P., & Boronat, C. (2001). Metaphor is like analogy. In D. Gentner, K. J. Holyoak, & B. N. Kokinov (Eds.), *The analogical mind: Perspectives from cognitive science* (pp. 199-253). Cambridge, MA: MIT Press.

Gentner, D., & France, I. M. (1988). The verb mutability effect: Studies of the combinatorial semantics of nouns and verbs. In S. L. Small, G. W. Cottrell, & M. K. Tanenhaus (Eds.), *Lexical ambiguity resolution: Perspectives from psycholinguistics, neuropsychology, and artificial intelligence* (pp. 343-382). San Mateo, CA: Morgan Kaufmann.

Gentner, D., & Kurtz, K. (2005). Relational categories. In W. K. Ahn, R. L. Goldstone, B. C. Love, A. B. Markman & P. W. Wolff (Eds.), *Categorization inside and outside the lab.* (pp. 151-175). Washington, DC: APA.

Gentner, D., & Wolff, P. (1997). Alignment in the processing of metaphor. *Journal of Memory and Language, 37*, 331-355.

Goatly, A. (2011). *The language of metaphors* (2nd ed.). London: Routledge.

Goldwater, M. B., Markman, A. B, Stilwell, C. H. (2011). The empirical case for role-governed categories. *Cognition, 118,* 359-376.

Goldwater, M. B., & Willits, J. (2010). *The Linguistic Distribution of Relational Categories.* Poster presented at the 32nd annual conference of the Cognitive Science Society, Portland, Oregon.

Kersten, A.W., & Earles, J.L. (2004). Semantic context influences memory for verbs more than memory for nouns. *Memory & Cognition, 32*, 198-211.

Lakoff, G., & Johnson, M. (1980). *Metaphors we live by*. Chicago, IL: The University of Chicago Press.

Markman, A. B., & Stilwell, C. H. (2001). Role-governed categories. *Journal of Experimental & Theoretical Intelligence, 13*, 329-358.

Reddy, M. J. (1979). The conduit metaphor: A case of frame conflict in our language about language. In A. Ortony (Ed.), *Metaphor and thought, 1st ed.* (pp. 284-324). Cambridge, England: Cambridge University Press.

Shutova, E., & Teufel, S. (2010). Metaphor corpus annotated for source-target domain mappings. *Proceedings of LREC 2010*, 3255-3261.

Shutova, E., Teufel, S. & Korhonen, A. (2012). Statistical metaphor processing. *Computational Linguistics, 39*(2), 1-53.

Steen, G.J., Dorst, A.G., Herrmann, J.B., Kaal, A.A., Krennmayr, T., & Pasma, T. (2010). *A method for linguistic metaphor identification: From MIP to MIPVU.* Philadelphia: John Benjamins.

Traugott, E. C. (2004). Semantic Change. In K. Brown (Ed.) *Encyclopedia of Language and Linguistics* (2nd ed.). Oxford: Elsevier.

Zharikov, S., & Gentner, D. (2002). Why do metaphors seem deeper than similes? *Proceedings of the Twenty-Fourth Annual Conference of the Cognitive Science Society*, 976-981.

Semantic Signatures for Example-Based Linguistic Metaphor Detection

Michael Mohler and **David Bracewell** and **David Hinote** and **Marc Tomlinson**
Language Computer Corp.
Richardson, Texas, USA
{michael,david,dhinote,marc}@languagecomputer.com

Abstract

Metaphor is a pervasive feature of human language that enables us to conceptualize and communicate abstract concepts using more concrete terminology. Unfortunately, it is also a feature that serves to confound a computer's ability to comprehend natural human language. We present a method to detect linguistic metaphors by inducing a domain-aware semantic signature for a given text and compare this signature against a large index of known metaphors. By training a suite of binary classifiers using the results of several semantic signature-based rankings of the index, we are able to detect linguistic metaphors in unstructured text at a significantly higher precision as compared to several baseline approaches.

1 Introduction

Metaphor is a widely-used literary mechanism which allows for the comparison of seemingly unrelated concepts. It has been thoroughly studied in both the linguistics literature (Ahrens et al., 2003; Lakoff and Johnson, 1980; Tourangeau and Sternberg, 1982; Wilks, 1978) and more recently within the field of computational linguistics.[1] Although there have been many influential theories regarding the cognitive basis of metaphor, the most prominent among them is Lakoff's Contemporary Theory of Metaphor (Lakoff and Johnson, 1980; Lakoff, 1993), which popularized the idea of a *conceptual metaphor mapping*. Within the cognitive framework of a given conceptual mapping, terms pertaining to one concept or domain (the *source*) can be used figuratively to express some aspect of another concept or domain (the *target*). For example, the conceptual metaphor "Life is a Journey" indicates a medium within which the target concept "life" may be more easily discussed and understood. This particular mapping allows us to speak of one being stuck in a "dead-end" job, a crucial decision as being a "fork in the road", or someone's life "taking a wrong turn".

By allowing us to discuss an abstract target concept using the vocabulary and world knowledge associated with a more familiar source concept, metaphor serves as a vehicle for human communication and understanding, and as such, has been found to be extremely prevalent in natural language, occurring as often as every third sentence (Shutova et al., 2010). As a consequence of this ubiquity, it is crucial that any system tasked with the understanding of natural language be capable of detecting the presence of metaphor in text and of modeling the intended semantic content of the metaphoric expression. In this work, we first induce a domain-sensitive semantic signature which we define as a set of highly related and interlinked WordNet (Fellbaum, 1998) senses drawn and augmented from a text that may be used to place the text within the semantic space of a metaphoric concept. We then employ a suite of binary classifiers to detect metaphoricity within a text by comparing its semantic signature to a set of known metaphors. If the semantic signature of the text closely matches the signature of a known metaphor, we propose that it is likely to represent

[1] For a broad survey of the relevant literature, see Shutova (2010).

Example	Metaphor
Obama heard a bomb ticking in his left ear.	No
Obama heard another political bomb ticking, this time in his left ear.	Yes

Table 1: The top sentence describes a literal bomb ticking, while the bottom sentence uses metaphoric language to describe an impending political disaster.

an instance of the same conceptual metaphor. To facilitate this work, we have built an index of known metaphors within a particular target domain. We have selected the domain of *Governance* which we define broadly to include electoral politics, the setting and enactment of economic policy, and the creation, application, and enforcement of rules and laws.

The problem of metaphor as it relates to computer understanding is illustrated in the example sentences of Table 1. A strictly literal reading suggests that the two sentences are describing something very similar. At the very least, the semantics of the phrases "bomb ticking" and "in his left ear" are indistinguishable without the added knowledge that the second sentence is using metaphor to convey information about something altogether different from explosives and body parts. From the context of the full sentences, it is clear that while the first sentence is straightforwardly describing Obama and his perception of a literal bomb, the second is describing an impending political crisis as though it were a bomb. Rather than a literal "ear" this sentence uses the phrase "in his left ear" to suggest that the source of the crisis in on the political "left". In order for an automated system to correctly understand the intended meaning of these sentences, it must first be aware that the text under consideration is not to be taken literally, and given this knowledge, it must employ all available knowledge of the underlying conceptual mapping to appropriately interpret the text in context.

The remainder of this work is organized as follows. In Section 2, we survey related work in semantic representation and linguistic metaphor identification. Section 3 describes in detail our approach to metaphor identification through the use of semantic signatures. In Section 4, we discuss the setup of our experiment which includes the creation of our metaphor index as well as the extraction and annotation of our training and testing data sets. Finally, we show the results of our experiments in Section 5 and share our conclusions in Section 6.

2 Related Work

The phenomenon of metaphor has been studied by researchers across multiple disciplines, including psychology, linguistics, sociology, anthropology, and computational linguistics. A number of theories of metaphor have been proposed, including the Contemporary Theory of Metaphor (Lakoff, 1993), the Conceptual Mapping Model (Ahrens et al., 2003), the Structure Mapping Model (Wolff and Gentner, 2000), and the Attribute Categorization Hypothesis (McGlone, 1996). Based on these theories, large collections of metaphors have been assembled and published for use by researchers. The Master Metaphor List (MML) (Lakoff, 1994) groups linguistic metaphors together according to their conceptual mapping, and the Hamburg Metaphor Database (HMD) (Eilts and Lönneker, 2002) for French and German fuses EuroWordNet synsets with the MML source and target domains for a robust source of metaphoric semantics in those languages.

In recent years, the computational linguistics community has seen substantial activity in the detection of figurative language (Bogdanova, 2010; Li and Sporleder, 2010; Peters and Wilks, 2003; Shutova, 2011) one aspect of which is the identification of metaphoric expressions in text (Fass, 1991; Shutova et al., 2010; Mason, 2004). Much of the early work on the identification of metaphor relied upon hand-crafted world knowledge. The met* (Fass, 1991) system sought to determine whether an expression was literal or figurative by detecting the violation of selectional preferences. Figurative expressions were then classified as either metonymic, using hand-crafted patterns, or metaphoric, using a manually constructed database of analogies. The CorMet (Mason, 2004) system determined the source and target concepts of a metaphoric expression using domain-specific selectional preferences mined from Internet resources. More recent work has examined noun-verb clustering (Shutova et al., 2010) which starts from a small seed set of one-word metaphors and results in clusters that represent source and target concepts connected via a metaphoric relation. These clusters are then used to annotate the metaphoricity of text.

Similar to our work, the Metaphor Interpretation, Denotation, and Acquisition System (MIDAS) (Martin, 1990) employed a database of conventional metaphors that could be searched to find a match for a metaphor discovered in text. If no match was found, the metaphoric text was replaced with a more abstract equivalent (e.g. a hypernym) and the database was searched again. If a match was found, an interpretation mapping was activated, and the novel metaphor would be added to the database for use in future encounters. Unfortunately, this technique was limited to interpreting known metaphors (and descendants of known metaphors) and was unable to detect truly novel usages. By expanding the metaphors using a more robust semantic signature, we attempt to transcend this limitation thereby producing a more durable system for metaphoric example linking.

An additional vein of metaphor research has sought to model the human processing of metaphor as a semantic space within which source and target concepts can be placed such that the similarity between their representations within this space (i.e. semantic vectors) can be sensibly quantified (Katz, 1992; Utsumi, 2011). One computational example of this approach (Kintsch, 2000) has employed latent semantic analysis (LSA) (Landauer and Dumais, 1997) to represent the semantic space of the metaphors in a reduced dimensionality (i.e. using singular value decomposition). In their approach, metaphors were represented as a set of terms found using a spreading activation algorithm informed by the terms' independent vector relatedness to the source and target concepts within some LSA space. By contrast, we have chosen to represent the metaphoric space using WordNet senses which have been shown in previous work(Lönneker, 2003) to represent a viable representation language for metaphor. We believe that the ontological knowledge encoded in the semantic relationships of WordNet represents an improvement over the distributional relatedness encoded within an LSA vector.

Also of relevance to the construction and use of semantic signatures is current research on the induction of topic signatures. A topic signature is a set of related words with associated weights which define and indicate the distinct topics within a text. In their work on automated summarization, Lin and Hovy (2000) developed a method for the construction of topic signatures which were mined from a large corpus. Similarly, Harabagiu and Lacatusu (2005) explored the use of topic signatures and enhanced topic signatures for their work on multi-document summarization. By contrast, we explore the use of semantic signatures which serve to enrich the semantics of the source and target frame concepts being expressed in a text for the purpose of detecting the presence of metaphor.

3 Methodology

In this work, we approach the task of linguistic metaphor detection as a classification problem. Starting from a known target domain (i.e. *Governance*), we first produce a target domain signature which represents the target-specific dimensions of the full conceptual space. Using this domain signature, we are able to separate the individual terms of a sentence into source frame elements and target frame elements and to independently perform a semantic expansion for each set of elements using WordNet and Wikipedia as described in our earlier work (Bracewell et al., 2013). Taken together, the semantic expansions of a text's source frame elements and target frame elements make up the full semantic signature of the text which can then be compared to an index of semantic signatures generated for a collection of manually detected metaphors. We use as features for our classifiers a set of metrics that are able to quantify the similarity between the given semantic signature and the signatures of metaphors found within the index.

3.1 Constructing a Target Domain Signature

In order to produce a semantic representation of the text, we first build a target domain signature, which we define as a set of highly related and interlinked

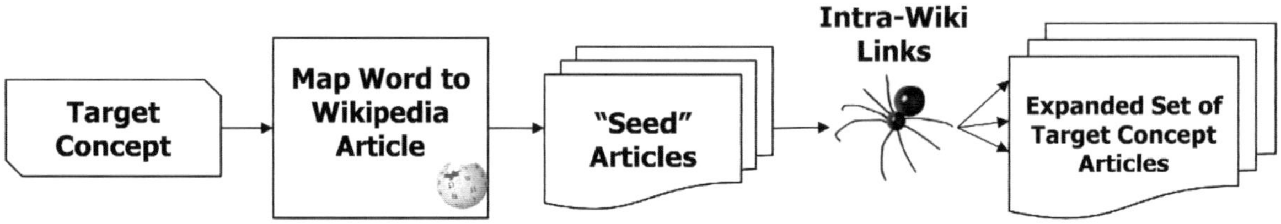

Figure 1: Focused crawling of Wikipedia articles pertaining to the target concept using intra-wiki links

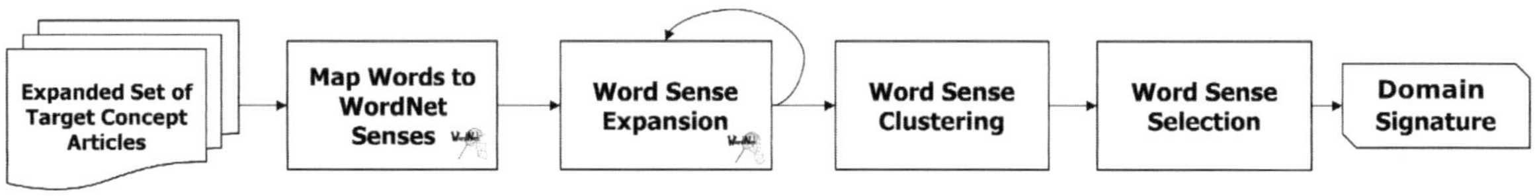

Figure 2: Constructing the domain signature of the target concept from Wikipedia articles pertaining to the target concept

WordNet senses that correspond to our particular target domain with statistical reliability. For example, in the domain of *Governance* the concepts of "law", "government", and "administrator", along with their associated senses in WordNet, are present in the domain signature. We generate this signature using semantic knowledge encoded in the following resources: (1) the semantic network encoded in WordNet; (2) the semantic structure implicit in Wikipedia; and (3) collocation statistics taken from the statistical analysis of a large corpora. In particular, we use Wikipedia as an important source of world knowledge which is capable of providing information about concepts, such as named entities, that are not found in WordNet as shown in several recent studies (Toral et al., 2009; Niemann and Gurevych, 2011). For example, the organization "Bilderberg Group" is not present in WordNet, but can easily be found in Wikipedia where it is listed under such categories as "Global trade and professional organizations", "International business", and "International non-governmental organizations". From these categories we can determine that the "Bilderberg Group" is highly related to WordNet senses such as "professional organization", "business", "international", and "nongovernmental organization".

We begin our construction of the domain signature by utilizing the semantic markup in Wikipedia to collect articles that are highly related to the target concept by searching for the target concept (and optionally content words making up the definition of the target concept) in the Wikipedia article titles and redirects. These articles then serve as a "seed set" for a Wikipedia crawl over the intra-wiki links present in the articles. By initiating the crawl on these links, it becomes focused on the particular domain expressed in the seed articles. The crawling process continues until either no new articles are found or a predefined crawl depth (from the set of seed articles) has been reached. The process is illustrated in Figure 1. The result of the crawl is a set of Wikipedia articles whose domain is related to the target concept. From this set of articles, the domain signature can be built by exploiting the semantic information provided by WordNet.

The process of going from a set of target concept articles to a domain signature is illustrated in Figure 2 and begins by associating the terms contained in the gathered Wikipedia articles with all of their possible WordNet senses (i.e. no word sense disambiguation is performed). The word senses are then expanded using the lexical (e.g. derivationally related forms) and semantic relations (e.g. hypernym and hyponym) available in WordNet. These senses are then clustered to eliminate irrelevant senses using the graph-based Chinese Whispers algorithm (Biemann, 2006). We transform our collection of word senses into a graph by treating each word sense as a vertex of an undirected, fully-connected graph where edge weights are taken to be the product of the Hirst and St-Onge (1998) WordNet similarity between the two word senses and the first-order corpus cooccurrence of the two terms. In particular, we use the normalized pointwise mutual information as computed using a web-scale corpus.

The clusters resulting from the Chinese Whispers algorithm contain semantically and topically similar word senses such that the size of a cluster is directly proportional to the centrality of the concepts within the cluster as they pertain to the target domain. After removing stopwords from the clusters, any clusters below a predefined size are removed. Any cluster with a low[2] average normalized pointwise mutual information (npmi) score between the word senses in the cluster and the word senses in the set of terms related to the target are likewise removed. This set of target-related terms used in calculating the npmi are constructed from the gathered Wikipedia articles using TF-IDF (term frequency inverse document frequency), where TF is calculated within the gathered articles and IDF is calculated using the entire textual content of Wikipedia. After pruning clusters based on size and score, the set of word senses that remain are taken to be the set of concepts that make up the target domain signature.

3.2 Building Semantic Signatures for Unstructured Text

After constructing a signature that defines the domain of the target concept, it is possible to use this signature to map a given text (e.g. a sentence) into a multidimensional conceptual space which allows us to compare two texts directly based on their conceptual similarity. This process begins by mapping the words of the text into WordNet and extracting the four most frequent senses for each term. In order to improve coverage and to capture entities and terms not found in WordNet, we also map terms to Wikipedia articles based on a statistical measure which considers both the text of the article and the intra-wiki links. The Wikipedia articles are then mapped back to WordNet senses using the text of the categories associated with the article.

In the next step, source and target frame elements of a given text are separated using the WordNet senses contained in the target domain signature. Terms in the text which have some WordNet sense that is included in the domain signature are classified as target frame elements while those that do not are considered source frame elements. Figure 3 shows an overview of the process for determining the source and target concepts within a text. The remainder of the signature induction process is performed separately for the source and target frame elements. In both cases, the senses are expanded using the lexical and semantic relations encoded in WordNet, including hypernymy, domain categories, and pertainymy. Additionally, source frame elements are expanded using the content words found in the glosses associated with each of the noun and verb senses. Taken together, these concepts represent the dimensions of a full conceptual space which can be separately expressed as the source concept dimensions and target concept dimensions of the space.

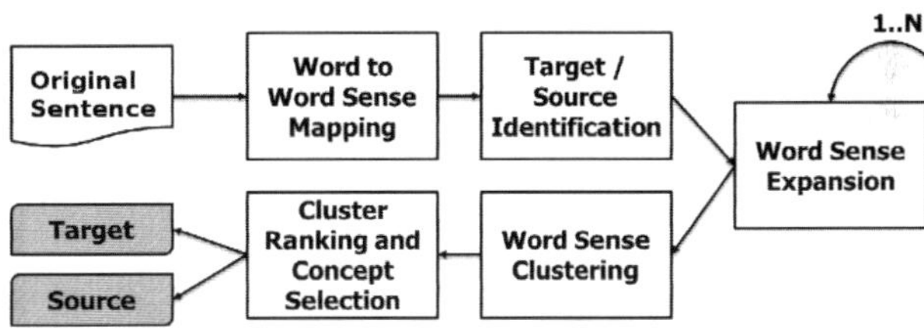

Figure 3: Example of a generated conceptual space for a given text. In this work, only one iteration of the sense expansion is performed.

In order to determine the correct senses for inclusion in the semantic signature of a text, clustering is performed using the same methodology as in the construction of the domain signature. First, a graph is built from the senses with edge weights assigned based on WordNet similarity and cooccurrence. Then, the Chinese Whispers algorithm is used to cluster the graph which serves to disambiguate the senses and to prioritize which senses are examined and incorporated into the source concept dimensions of the conceptual space. Word senses are prioritized by ranking the clusters based on their size and on the highest scoring word sense contained in the cluster using:

$$rank(c) = size(c) \cdot \left(\frac{\sum_s score(s)}{|c|} \right) \quad (1)$$

where c is the cluster, s is a word sense in the clus-

[2]We define low as being below an empirically defined threshold, τ.

ter, and $|c|$ is the total number of word senses in the cluster. The senses are scored using: (1) the degree distribution of the sense in the graph (more central word senses are given a higher weight); and (2) the length of the shortest path to the terms appearing in the given text with concepts closer to the surface form given a higher weight. Formally, $score(s)$ is calculated as:

$$score(s) = \frac{degree(s) + dijkstra(s, R)}{2} \quad (2)$$

where $degree(s)$ is degree distribution of s and $dijkstra(s, R)$ is the length of the shortest path in the graph between s and some term in the original text, R.

Clusters containing only one word sense or with a score less than the average cluster score (μ_c) are ignored. The remaining clusters and senses are then examined for incorporation into the conceptual space with senses contained in higher ranked clusters examined first. Senses are added as concepts within the conceptual space when their score is greater than the average word sense score (μ_s). To decrease redundancy in the dimensions of the conceptual space, neighbors of the added word sense in the graph are excluded from future processing.

3.3 Classification

Given a semantic signature representing the placement of a text within our conceptual space, it is possible to measure the conceptual distance to other signatures within the same space. By mapping a set of known metaphors into this space (using the process described in Section 3.2), we can estimate the likelihood that a given text contains some metaphor (within the same target domain) by using the semantic signature of the text to find the metaphors with the most similar signatures and to measure their similarity with the original signature.

We quantify this similarity using five related measures which are described in Table 2. Each of these features involves producing a score that ranks every metaphor in the index based upon the semantic signature of the given text in a process similar to that of traditional information retrieval. In particular, we use the signature of the text to build a query against which the metaphors can be scored. For each word sense included in the semantic signature, we add a clause to the query which combines the vector space model with the Boolean model so as to prefer a high overlap of senses without requiring an identical match between the signatures.[3]

Three of the features simply take the score of the highest ranked metaphor as returned by a query. Most simply, the feature labeled *Max Score (naïve)* uses the full semantic signature for the text which should serve to detect matches that are very similar in both the source concept dimensions and the target concept dimensions. The features *Max Score (source)* and *Max Score (target)* produce the query using only the source concept dimensions of the signature and the target concept dimensions respectively.

The remaining two features score the metaphors within the source dimensions and the target dimensions separately before combining the results into a joint score. The feature *Max Score (joint)* calculates the product of the scores for each metaphor using the source- and target-specific queries described above and selects the maximum value among these products. The final feature, *Joint Count*, represents the total number of metaphors with a score for both the source and the target dimensions above some threshold (μ_j). Unlike the more naïve features for which a very good score in one set of dimensions may incorrectly lead to a high overall score, these joint similarity features explicitly require metaphors to match the semantic signature of the text within both the source and target dimensions simultaneously.

Altogether, these five features are used to train a suite of binary classifiers to make a decision on whether a given text is or is not a metaphor.

4 Experimental Setup

One crucial component of our linguistic metaphor detection system is the index of metaphors (in the domain of *Governance*) against which we compare our candidate texts. As a part of this project, we have produced an ever-growing, metaphor-rich dataset taken from political speeches, political websites (e.g. Communist Party USA, Tea Party sites,

[3]This functionality comes standard with the search functionality of Apache Lucene which we employ for the production of our index.

Measure	Description
Max Score (naïve)	Find the score of the metaphor that best matches the full semantic signature
Max Score (source)	Find the score of the metaphor that best matches the source side of the semantic signature
Max Score (target)	Find the score of the metaphor that best matches the target side of the semantic signature
Max Score (joint)	Independently score the metaphors by the target side and by the source side. Find the metaphor with the highest product of the scores.
Joint Count	Independently score the metaphors by the target side and by the source side. Count the number of metaphors that receive a positive score for both.

Table 2: The five features used by our metaphoricity classifiers.

etc.), and political commentary in web-zines and online newspapers. Three annotators have analyzed the raw texts and manually selected snippets of text (with context) whenever some element in the text seemed to have been used figuratively to describe or stand in for another element not represented in the text.[4] Each of these metaphors is projected into a conceptual space using the process described in Section 3.2 and assembled into a searchable index.

For evaluation purposes, we have selected a subset of our overall repository which consists of 500 raw documents that have been inspected for metaphoricity by our annotators. We allocate 80% of these documents for the training of our classifiers and evaluate using the remaining 20%. In total, our training data consists of 400 documents containing 1,028 positive examples of metaphor and around 16,000 negative examples. Our test set consists of 100 documents containing 4,041 sentences with 241 positive examples of metaphor and 3,800 negative examples. For each sentence in each document, our system attempts to determine whether the sentence does or does not contain a metaphor within the domain of *Governance*.

We have experimented with several flavors of machine learning classification. In addition to an in-house implementation of a binary maximum entropy (MaxEnt) classifier, we have evaluated our results using four separate classifiers from the popular Weka machine learning toolkit.[5] These include an unpruned decision tree classifier (J48), a support vector machine (SMO) approach using a quadratic kernel with parameters tuned via grid search, a rule-based approach (JRIP), and a random forest classifier (RF). In addition, we have combined all five classifiers into an ensemble classifier which uses a uniformly-weighted voting methodology to arrive at a final decision.

5 Results

We have evaluated our methodology in two ways. First, we have performed an evaluation which highlights the discriminatory capabilities of our features by testing on a balanced subset of our test data. Next, we performed an evaluation which shows the utility of each of our classifiers as they are applied to real world data with a natural skew towards literal usages.[6] In both cases, we train on a balanced subset of our training data using all 1,028 positive examples and a set of negative examples selected randomly such that each document under consideration contains the same number of positive and negative examples. In an initial experiment, we trained our classifiers on the full (skewed) training data, but the results suggested that an error-minimizing strategy would lead to all sentences being classified as "literal".

As shown in Table 3, the choice of classifier appears significant. Several of the classifiers (J48, JRIP, and MaxEnt) maintain a high recall suggesting the ability of the tree- and rule-based classifiers to reliably "filter out" non-metaphors. On the other hand, other classifiers (SMO and ENSEMBLE) operate in a mode of high precision suggesting that a high confidence can be associated with their positive classifications. In all cases, performance is signifi-

[4]Generally speaking, each annotator operated within a region of high precision and low recall, and the overlap between individual annotators was low. As such, we have selected the union of all metaphors detected by the annotators.

[5]http://www.cs.waikato.ac.nz/ml/weka/

[6]Note that metaphors that are not related to the domain of *Governance* are classified as "literal".

Classifier	Precision	Recall	F-Measure
J48	56.1%	93.0%	70.0%
JRIP	57.7%	79.3%	66.8%
MaxEnt	59.9%	72.6%	65.7%
ENSEMBLE	72.0%	42.7%	53.7%
RF	55.8%	47.7%	51.5%
SMO	75.0%	33.6%	46.4%
All metaphor	50.0%	100.0%	66.7%
Random baseline	50.0%	50.0%	50.0%

Table 3: The results of our experiments using several machine learning classifiers while evaluating on a dataset with 241 positive examples and 241 negative examples.

Classifier	Precision	Recall	F-Measure
SMO	12.7%	33.6%	18.4%
ENSEMBLE	11.2%	42.7%	17.8%
MaxEnt	8.7%	72.6%	15.6%
JRIP	8.1%	79.3%	14.8%
J48	7.6%	93.0%	14.0%
RF	7.4%	47.7%	12.7%
All metaphor	6.0%	100.0%	11.3%
Random baseline	6.0%	50.0%	10.7%

Table 4: The results of our experiments using several machine learning classifiers while evaluating on naturally skewed dataset with 241 positive examples and 3,800 negative examples.

cantly better than chance as reported by our random baseline.[7]

Table 4 shows the result of evaluating the same models on an unbalanced dataset with a natural skew towards "literal" sentences which reflects a more realistic use case in the context of linguistic metaphor detection. The results suggest that, once again, the decision tree classification accepts the vast majority of all metaphors (93%), but also produces a significant number of false positives making it difficult to usefully employ this classifier as a complete metaphor detection system despite its top-performing F-measure on the balanced dataset. More useful is the SMO approach, which shows a precision over twice that of the random baseline. Put another way, a positive result from this classifier is more than 110% more likely to be correct than a random classification. From the standpoint of utility, joining these classifiers in an ensemble configuration seems to combine the high precision of the SMO classifier with the improved recall of the other classifiers making the ensemble configuration a viable choice in a real world scenario.

6 Conclusions

We have shown in this work the potential utility of our example-based approach to detect metaphor within a domain by comparing the semantic signature of a text with a set of known metaphors. Although this technique is necessarily limited by the coverage of the metaphors in the index, we believe that it is a viable technique for metaphor detection as more and more examples become available. In future work, we hope to supplement our existing features with such information as term imageability, the transmission of affect, and selectional preference violation we believe will result in a robust system for linguistic metaphor detection to further aid in the computer understanding of natural language.

[7] According to Fisher's exact test (one-tailed): RF ($p < 0.02$); all others ($p < 0.0001$).

Acknowledgments

This research is supported by the Intelligence Advanced Research Projects Activity (IARPA) via Department of Defense US Army Research Laboratory contract number W911NF-12-C-0025. The U.S. Government is authorized to reproduce and distribute reprints for Governmental purposes notwithstanding any copyright annotation thereon. Disclaimer: The views and conclusions contained herein are those of the authors and should not be interpreted as necessarily representing the official policies or endorsements, either expressed or implied, of IARPA, DoD/ARL, or the U.S. Government. We would also like to thank our annotators whose efforts have made this work possible.

References

K. Ahrens, S.F. Chung, and C. Huang. 2003. Conceptual metaphors: Ontology-based representation and corpora driven mapping principles. In *Proceedings of the ACL 2003 workshop on Lexicon and figurative language-Volume 14*, pages 36–42. Association for Computational Linguistics.

C. Biemann. 2006. Chinese whispers: an efficient graph clustering algorithm and its application to natural language processing problems. In *Proceedings of the First Workshop on Graph Based Methods for Natural Language Processing*, pages 73–80. Association for Computational Linguistics.

D. Bogdanova. 2010. A framework for figurative language detection based on sense differentiation. In *Proceedings of the ACL 2010 Student Research Workshop*, pages 67–72. Association for Computational Linguistics.

D. Bracewell, M. Tomlinson, and M. Mohler. 2013. Determining the conceptual space of metaphoric expressions. In *Computational Linguistics and Intelligent Text Processing*, pages 487–500. Springer.

C. Eilts and B. Lönneker. 2002. The Hamburg Metaphor Database.

D. Fass. 1991. met*: A method for discriminating metonymy and metaphor by computer. *Computational Linguistics*, 17(1):49–90.

C. Fellbaum. 1998. *WordNet, An Electronic Lexical Database*. The MIT Press.

S. Harabagiu and F. Lacatusu. 2005. Topic themes for multi-document summarization. In *Proceedings of the 28th annual international ACM SIGIR conference on Research and development in information retrieval*, pages 202–209. ACM.

G. Hirst and D. St-Onge. 1998. Lexical chains as representations of context for the detection and correction of malapropism. In Christiane Fellbaum, editor, *WordNet: An Electronic Lexical Database*, pages 305–332. MIT Press.

A.N. Katz. 1992. Psychological studies in metaphor processing: extensions to the placement of terms in semantic space. *Poetics Today*, pages 607–632.

W. Kintsch. 2000. Metaphor comprehension: A computational theory. *Psychonomic Bulletin & Review*, 7(2):257–266.

G. Lakoff and M. Johnson. 1980. *Metaphors we live by*, volume 111. Chicago London.

G. Lakoff. 1993. The contemporary theory of metaphor. *Metaphor and thought*, 2:202–251.

G. Lakoff. 1994. *Master metaphor list*. University of California.

T.K. Landauer and S.T. Dumais. 1997. A solution to Plato's problem: The latent semantic analysis theory of acquisition, induction, and representation of knowledge. *Psychological Review; Psychological Review*, 104(2):211.

L. Li and C. Sporleder. 2010. Using gaussian mixture models to detect figurative language in context. In *Human Language Technologies: The 2010 Annual Conference of the North American Chapter of the Association for Computational Linguistics*, pages 297–300. Association for Computational Linguistics.

C. Lin and E. Hovy. 2000. The automated acquisition of topic signatures for text summarization. In *Proceedings of the 18th conference on Computational linguistics-Volume 1*, pages 495–501. Association for Computational Linguistics.

B. Lönneker. 2003. Is there a way to represent metaphors in WordNets?: insights from the Hamburg Metaphor Database. In *Proceedings of the ACL 2003 workshop on Lexicon and figurative language-Volume 14*, pages 18–27. Association for Computational Linguistics.

J.H. Martin. 1990. *A computational model of metaphor interpretation*. Academic Press Professional, Inc.

Z.J. Mason. 2004. CorMet: A computational, corpus-based conventional metaphor extraction system. *Computational Linguistics*, 30(1):23–44.

M.S. McGlone. 1996. Conceptual metaphors and figurative language interpretation: Food for thought? *Journal of memory and language*, 35(4):544–565.

E. Niemann and I. Gurevych. 2011. The people's web meets linguistic knowledge: Automatic sense alignment of Wikipedia and WordNet. In *Proceedings of the 9th International Conference on Computational Semantics (IWCS)*, pages 205–214. Citeseer.

W. Peters and Y. Wilks. 2003. Data-driven detection of figurative language use in electronic language resources. *Metaphor and Symbol*, 18(3):161–173.

E. Shutova, L. Sun, and A. Korhonen. 2010. Metaphor identification using verb and noun clustering. In *Proceedings of the 23rd International Conference on Computational Linguistics*, pages 1002–1010. Association for Computational Linguistics.

E. Shutova. 2010. Models of metaphor in NLP. In *Proceedings of the 48th Annual Meeting of the Association for Computational Linguistics*, pages 688–697. Association for Computational Linguistics.

E.V. Shutova. 2011. *Computational approaches to figurative language*. Ph.D. thesis, University of Cambridge.

S.L. Toral, M.R. Martínez-Torres, F. Barrero, and F. Cortés. 2009. An empirical study of the driving forces behind online communities. *Internet Research*, 19(4):378–392.

R. Tourangeau and R.J. Sternberg. 1982. Understanding and appreciating metaphors. *Cognition*, 11(3):203–244.

A. Utsumi. 2011. Computational exploration of metaphor comprehension processes using a semantic space model. *Cognitive science*, 35(2):251–296.

Y. Wilks. 1978. Making preferences more active. *Artificial Intelligence*, 11(3):197–223.

P. Wolff and D. Gentner. 2000. Evidence for role-neutral initial processing of metaphors. *Journal of Experimental Psychology: Learning, Memory, and Cognition*, 26(2):529.

Automatic Metaphor Detection using Large-Scale Lexical Resources and Conventional Metaphor Extraction

Yorick Wilks, Lucian Galescu, James Allen, Adam Dalton
Florida Institute for Human and Machine Cognition
15, SE Osceola Ave
Ocala, FL, 34471, USA
{ywilks,lgalescu,jallen,adalton}@ihmc.us

Abstract

The paper presents an experimental algorithm to detect conventionalized metaphors implicit in the lexical data in a resource like WordNet, where metaphors are coded into the senses and so would never be detected by any algorithm based on the violation of preferences, since there would always be a constraint satisfied by such senses. We report an implementation of this algorithm, which was implemented first the preference constraints in VerbNet. We then derived in a systematic way a far more extensive set of constraints based on WordNet glosses, and with this data we reimplemented the detection algorithm and got a substantial improvement in recall. We suggest that this technique could contribute to improve the performance of existing metaphor detection strategies that do not attempt to detect conventionalized metaphors. The new WordNet-derived data is of wider significance because it also contains adjective constraints, unlike any existing lexical resource, and can be applied to any language with a semantic parser (and WN) for it.

1 Introduction

Metaphor is ubiquitous in standard language; it is not a fringe or add-on phenomenon. The work described concerns detecting and interpreting metaphor on a large scale in corpora. If metaphor is ubiquitous, then locating and interpreting it must be central to any NLP project that aims to understand general language. This paper focuses on the initial phase of detection: the identification in text of conceptual combinations that might be deemed metaphoric by a pre-theoretic observer, e.g., "*Brazil has economic muscle*", "*Tom is a brick*", or "*The unions have built a fortress round their pensions*". There is a long cultural tradition of describing and interpreting such phenomena but our goal here is computational: to provide criteria for automatically detecting such cases as candidates for further analysis and interpretation.

The key fact is that metaphors are sometimes new and fresh but can be immediately understood: producing them is often the role of poets, creative journalists and writers of all kinds. But many are simply part of the history of the language, and are novel only to those who do not happen to know them already: for example "*Tom is a brick*" – taken to mean that he is a reliable man, but which cannot be literally true – is actually encoded as a sense of *brick* in WordNet (WN) (Miller, 1995) even though it is more familiar to UK than US English speakers.

This means that lexical resources already contain conventionalized metaphors. We propose a simple method for locating and extracting these into the metaphor candidate pool, even when they are not indicated as such in resources like WN (which marks figurative senses very infrequently, unlike some traditional dictionaries). However, we believe these implicit metaphors in WN – a resource we intend to use as a semantic/lexical database, though transformed as we shall show below – can be extracted by a simple algorithm, and without any need for *a priori* distinction of literal versus metaphorical. That distinction, as we noted, depends to a large degree on the temporal snapshot of a language; e.g., no one now would think "*taking a decision*" was metaphor, even though decisions are not literally taken anywhere.

In this paper, we shall present an algorithm for conventionalized metaphor detection, and show results over a standard corpus of examples that demonstrate a possible useful gain in recall of metaphors, our original aim. The algorithm is described in two implementations (or pipelines) corresponding, respectively, to the use of WN and VerbNet (Kipper et al., 2000; Kipper et al., 2008) as semantic knowledge-bases, and to their replacement by our automatically recomputed form of WN, which enables predictions about the preference behavior (see below) of English verbs and adjectives to be better founded than in VerbNet (VN) and on a much larger scale.

2 Background on Metaphor Detection using Preference Violation as Cue

In early work on metaphor detection, long preceding access to large-scale or annotated corpora, it was suggested as sufficient a criterion for being a metaphor that a "semantic preference" of a verb or adjective was violated (Wilks, 1978). So, for example, one might say that the verb *drink* had a preference for animate agents and liquid objects, in which case "*My car drinks gasoline*" violates its subject preference, which might then be a cue to look for metaphor at that point. Similarly, in the "*economic muscle*" case mentioned earlier one might say that *economic* has a preference for abstract entities as objects, as in "*economic value*", and *muscle* is not an abstract entity.

There was discussion in those early days of syntactic-semantic interface cases like "*John ran a mile*" where *a mile* might be said to violate the preference of the (intransitive) verb for a zero object and so again trigger a metaphor. The preference notion was not initially intended to detect metaphor but to semantically disambiguate candidates at those sites by preferring those conceptual entities that did **not** violate such restrictions. In early work, preferences were largely derived by intuition and sometimes ordered by salience. Later (e.g. Resnik, 1997) there was a range of work on deriving such preferences from corpora; however, in VN the semantic preferences of verbs were again largely intuitive in origin.

Early work linking preference violation to metaphor detection (summarised in Fass and Wilks, 1983, also Martin 1990) worked with handcrafted resources, but by 1995 Dolan had noted (Dolan, 1995) that large-scale lexical resources would have implications for metaphor detection, and WN was used in conjunction with corpora, by (Peters and Wilks, 2003) using symbolic methods and by Mason (2004) and Krishnakumaran and Zhu (2007) using a combination of WN and statistical methods. Mason also acquires preferences automatically from corpora, and the latter two papers treat metaphor as a form of anomaly based on rare combinations of surface words and of WN-derived hypernyms, a notion that appears in (Guthrie et al., 2007) but based only on corpus sparsity and not WN codings. Other work on the automatic acquisition of preferences (McCarthy and Carrol, 2003) for WSD has also its considered extension to the detection of classes of metaphor. More recently, work by Shutova (Shutova et al., 2010) has shown that the original preference violation insight can be combined with large-scale investigations, using notions of machine learning and large-scale resources like WN. Our approach is smaller scale and does not involve machine learning: it simply seeks access to implicit metaphors built into the structure of WN by its creators, and which a preference-violation detection criterion cannot, by definition, access. Thus, we view our contribution as complementary to larger efforts on metaphor and interpretation detection, rather than a competing approach. We have not made comparisons here with the work of (Li and Sporleder, 2010), which is explicitly concerned with idioms, nor with (Markert and Nissim, 2009) which is focused on metonymy.

3 The Conventional Metaphor Detection Hypotheses

Where WN codes conventionalized metaphors as senses, as in the initial cases described, then the senses expressing these will NOT violate preferences and so will not be detected by any metaphor-as-violation hypothesis. For example, in "*Jane married a brick*" this will not be a preference violation against WN senses because WN explicitly codes *brick* as a reliable person, though we would almost certainly want to say this sentence contains a metaphor to be detected.

The hypothesis we propose is simply this: if we have a word whose main (usually first) sense in WN fails the main preference for the sentence slot it fills, but has a lower, less frequent, sense that satisfies that preference, then we declare that lower sense a metaphorical one. In the case of *brick*, whose main sense is a PHYSICAL OBJECT, one which clearly fails the equivalence to *Tom* in the example "*Tom is a brick*". Yet the less frequent listed sense for a reliable person does satisfy the same preference. The work at this stage is not concerned with the metaphor-metonymy distinction and this criterion may well capture both, their distinction being, as is well known (e.g. in Fass and Wilks, 1983) hard to establish in the limit. Ours is a purely empirical hypothesis and will work or not, and we argue that it does to a reasonable degree. It does not rest on any assumption of strict ordering of WN senses, only on a tendency (from literal to metaphorical) which is plainly there for any observer.

4 Metaphor Detection Experiments

We have implemented two versions of conventional metaphor detection, using two different lexical resources. We were thus able to divide the hypothesis into two parts, essentially one making use of VN and one within WN only. In this first pipeline, we use WN together with the verb preferences provided by VN even though those give only patchy coverage of common verbs. At the outset this was the only lexical resource for verb preferences available. VN includes classes of verbs that map members to specific WN senses. VN also provides a hierarchy of verb object/subject inclusions, which we use for assessing whether one sentence object/subject type appears below another in this simple inclusion hierarchy, and so can be said to be semantically included in it. The selectional restrictions, however, are not linked to any lexicons so a mapping was constructed in order to allow for automated detection of preference violations.

Our first experiment utilizes WN, VN, and the Stanford Parser (de Marneffe et al., 2006) and Named Entity Recognizer (Finkel et al., 2005). The Stanford Parser identifies the verbs, as well as their corresponding subjects and direct objects. The Stanford Named Entity Recognizer was used to replace sequences of text representing names with WN senses whose hypernyms exist in the selectional restriction hierarchy.

The first step in determining whether a sentence contains a metaphor is to extract all verbs along with the subject and direct object arguments for each verb. The Stanford Parser dependencies used to describe the relationships between verbs and their arguments include *agent, nsubj,* and *xsubj* for subjects and *dobj* and *nsubjpass* for direct objects. The parser also handles copular and prepositional verbs but additional steps are required to link these verbs to their arguments.

Once verbs have been extracted and parameterized from the sentence, each is checked for preference violations. A preference is violated if a selectional restriction on one of the thematic roles of a VN class is not satisfied for all VN classes the verb is a member of. In order for a VN class's preferences to be satisfied, there must be a WN sense for the argument of a verb such that either itself or its hypernym matches the WN senses allowed by the selectional restriction in VN class, where the terms in the VN hierarchy have been hand-matched to WN senses. If a sentence contains a verb that does not exist in VN then we must assume that it is not violated.

5 Conventionalized Metaphor Detection

Closer inspection of false negatives revealed that many of the verbs and the arguments that satisfied their selectional restrictions were unannotated conventionalized metaphors.

5.1 Conventionalized Verbs

In our approach, a conventionalized verb occurs when two VN Classes have the same member, but one maps to a lower WN sense (in the WN ordering, which can be taken roughly to mean less frequent) than the other. If the VN Class mapped to the lower sense is satisfied in a sentence, but the other VN Class is not, we say that the verb is used in a conventionalized sense. The verb *pour* is a member of four VN classes. Three of those classes, **Pour-9.5**, **Preparing-26.3-2**, and **Substance_Emission-43.4** all map to first sense of the word which means to *cause to run*. The fourth VN class of *pour*, **Weather-57,** maps to the sixth WN sense of the verb, which means *to rain heavily*. If we take the example sentence "*Bisciotti has poured money into the team*", we determine that all VN classes that map to the primary WN sense of *pour* are violated in some way. According to our semantic role labeling heuristic, **Pour-9.5** expects *money* to be a substance, **Preparing-26.3-2** expects *the team* to be an animate, and **Substance_Emission-43.4** is violated because Bisciotti is animate. The only Verb Class that is satisfied is

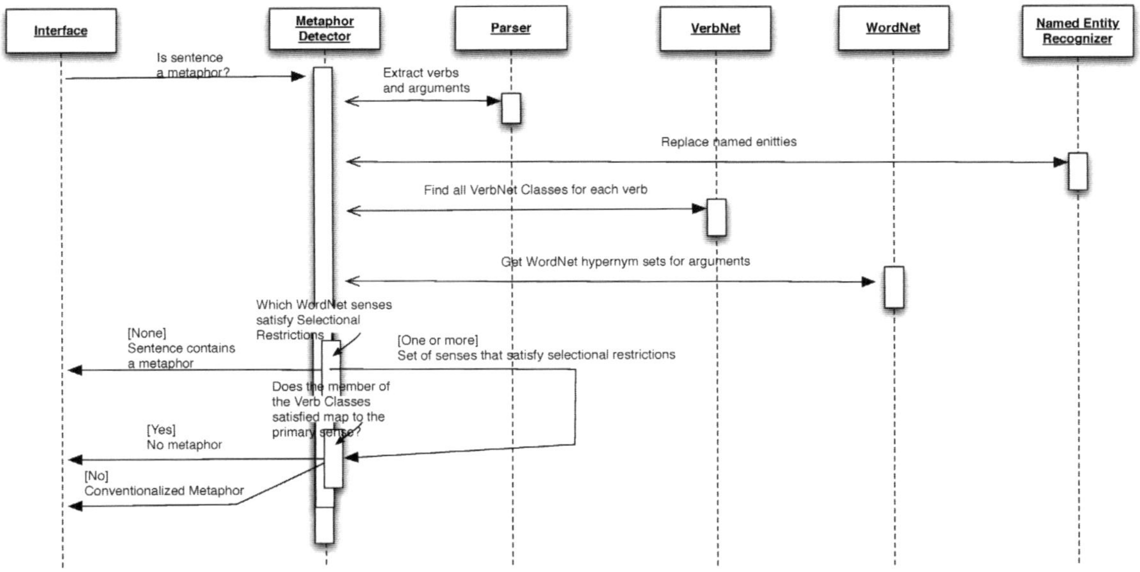

Figure 1. Conventionalized verb metaphor detection using WordNet senses and VerbNet selectional restrictions

Weather-57, and that class maps to the sixth sense of *pour*. Interestingly, there is no VN class member that maps to the fifth WN sense (*supply in large amounts or quantities*).

The pseudocode for detecting conventional metaphors used as verbs is as follows:

- for each VN Class
  - for each member of that class
    - for each WN sense of that member with Verb POS
      - get the sense number of the WN sense
      - associate the sense number to the verb member and selectional restrictions for the Verb Class
- given a verb in a sentence, decide that the verb is conventionalized if:
  - it satisfies the selectional restrictions of one Verb Class V_1 but...
  - it violates the selectional restrictions of another Verb Class V_2 and...
  - the sense number of the verb member in V_2 is above the sense number of the verb member in V_1

5.2 Conventionalized Nouns

Let us look again at the example of *brick*, where the primary sense of the noun is the building material most are familiar with and the secondary sense refers to a reliable person. For this reason, the noun *brick* will satisfy any VN class that requires a human or animate. Without the ability to detect conventional metaphors in noun arguments, *She married a brick* would pass through without detection by preference violation. Here are the WN entries for the two senses:

- **brick#1 (brick%1:06:00::)** (rectangular block of clay baked by the sun or in a kiln; used as a building or paving material)
- **brick#2 (brick%1:18:00::)** (a good fellow; helpful and trustworthy)

Less obvious are more abstract words such as *zone*:

- **zone#1** (**zone%1:15:00::**) (a locally circumscribed place characterized by some distinctive features)
- **zone#2** (**zone%1:15:02::**), **geographical zone#1 (geographical_zone%1:15:00::**) (any of the regions of the surface of the Earth loosely divided according to latitude or longitude)
- **zone#3 (zone%1:15:01::)** (an area or region distinguished from adjacent parts by a distinctive feature or characteristic)
- **zone#4 (zone%1:08:00::)**, **zona#1 (zona%1:08:00::)** ((anatomy) any encircling or beltlike structure)

Zone's primary sense, again, is the anticipated concept of circumscribed space. However, the fourth sense deals with anatomy, and therefore is a hyponym of *body part*. *Body part* is capable of satisfying any thematic role restricted to *animate* arguments.

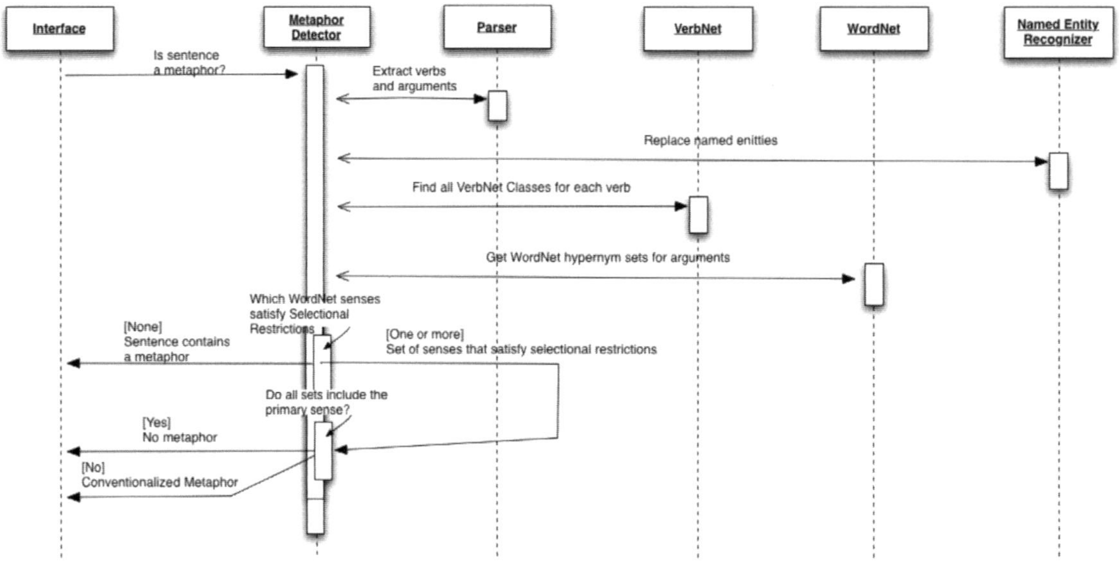

Figure 2. Conventionalized noun metaphor detection using WordNet senses and VerbNet selectional restrictions

The pseudocode for detecting conventional metaphors used as nouns is as follows:

```
• determine if verbs' subjects and di-
  rect objects satisfy the restriction
  • if not, it is a Preference Violation
    metaphor
  • if they do:
    • determine if the sense of the sat-
      isfying word is the primary sense
      in WN
      • if not, it is a conventional
        metaphor
      • otherwise, it is not a metaphor
```

Thus, our overall hypothesis is intended to locate in the very broad WN sense sets those that are actually conventionalized metaphors: we determine that only the first sense, hopefully literal, should be able to satisfy any restriction. If a lower sense satisfies a verb, but the primary sense does not, we classify the satisfaction as being conventionalized, but a metaphor nonetheless.

6 Deriving Preferences and an Ontology from WordNet

To date, VerbNet is the most extensive resource for verb roles and restrictions. It provides a rich semantic role taxonomy with some selectional restrictions. Still, VN has entries for less than 4000 verbs. PropBank (Palmer et al., 2005) has additional coverage, but uses a more surface oriented role set with no selectional restrictions. On the other hand, WordNet has many more verb entries but they lack semantic role information. However, we believe it is possible to extract automatically a comprehensive lexicon of verbs with semantic roles and selectional restrictions from WN by processing definitions in WN using deep understanding techniques. Specifically, each verb in WN comes with a gloss that defines the verb sense, and there we can find clues about the semantic roles and their selectional restrictions. Thus, we are testing the hypothesis that the semantic roles of the verb being defined are inherited from the roles in its definition, though roles in the latter may be elided or fully specified. For example, consider this entry from WN for one of the senses of the verb *kill*:

> S: (v) **kill** (cause to die; put to death, usually intentionally or knowingly) "*This man killed several people when he tried to rob the bank*"; "*the farmer killed a pig for the holidays*"

Let us assume we already know that the verb *cause* takes three roles, say, a CAUSER, an AFFECTED and an EFFECT role; this leads us to hypothesize that *kill* would take the same roles. However, the EFFECT role from cause is not inherited by *kill* as it is fully specified in the definition. The proof of

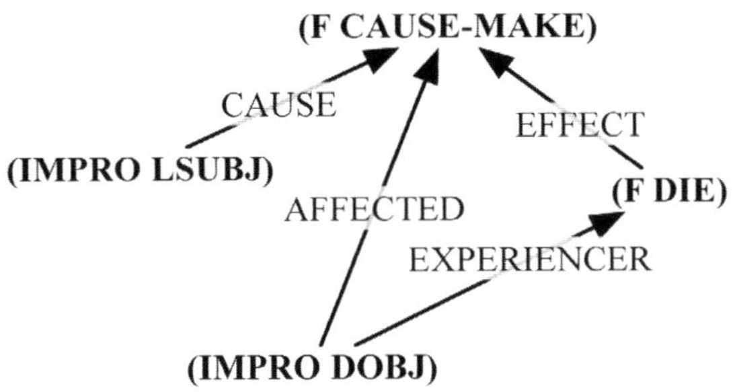

Figure 3: Abstracted Logical Form for "cause to die"

this hypothesis is ultimately in how well it predicts the role set. But intuitively, any role in the definition verb (i.e., *cause*) that is fully filled in the definition has no "space" for a new argument for that role. Therefore, we conclude that *kill* takes two roles, filling the CAUSER and AFFECTED roles in the definition.

We can now derive selectional restrictions for *kill* by looking at inherited restrictions from the definition, as well as those that can be derived from the examples. From the definition, the verb *cause* puts little to no restriction on what the CAUSER role might be. For instance, an animal may cause something, but natural forces cause things as well. Likewise, *cause* puts little constraint on what the PATIENT role might be, as one can cause the temperature to rise, or an idea to fade. The restriction from the verb *die* in the complement, however, suggests a restriction of some living object (if we can derive this constraint from *die*). We also look at the examples to find more informative restrictions. In the definition of *kill*, we have two examples of a CAUSER, namely a man and a farmer. Given the hypernym hierarchy of nouns in WordNet, we could look for the most specific subsuming concept in the hierarchy for the concepts MAN and FARMER, finding it to be **person%1:03:00**. The fillers for the AFFECTED role in the examples are PEOPLE and PIG, with the most specific WN node being **organism%1:03:00**). Putting all this together, we produce an entry for *kill* as follows:

kill: ACTOR/**person%1:03:00**
PATIENT/**organism%1:03:00**

To implement this idea we need a number of capabilities. First, semantic roles do not appear out of the ether, so we need an initial seed of semantic role information. In addition, to process the glosses we need a parser that can build a semantic representation, including the handling of elided arguments. As a start, we use the TRIPS parser (Allen et al., 2008). The TRIPS lexicon provides information on semantic roles, and the parser can construct the required semantic structures. TRIPS has been shown to be successful at parsing WN glosses in order to build commonsense knowledge bases (Allen et al., 2011). With around 3000 types, TRIPS offers a reasonable upper-level ontology to serve as the seed for semantic roles. We also use the TRIPS selectional restrictions to bootstrap the process of determining the restrictions for new words.

To attain broad lexical coverage, the TRIPS parser uses input from a variety of external resources. This includes a subsystem, Wordfinder, for unknown word lookup that accesses WN when an unknown word is encountered. The WN senses have mappings to semantic types in the TRIPS ontology, although sometimes at a fairly abstract level. When faced with an unknown word, the parser looks up the possible senses in WordNet, maps these to the TRIPS ontology and then uses the verb entries in the TRIPS lexicon associated with these types to suggest possible subcatgorization frames with mappings to roles. Thus, Wordfinder uses the combined information from WN and the TRIPS lexicon and ontology to dynamically build lexical entries with approximate semantic and syntactic structures for words not in the core lexicon. This process may produce a range of different possibilities based on the different senses and possible subcategorization frames for the verbs that share the same TRIPS type. We feed all of these to the parser and let it determine the entries that best match the definition and examples. While WordNet may have multiple fine-grained senses for a given word, we set a parameter that has the system use only the most frequent sense(s) of the word (cf. McCarthy et al. 2004).

We use TRIPS to parse the definitions and glosses into a logical form. Figure 3 shows the logical form produced for the definition *cause to die*. We then search the logical form for structures that signal a potential argument that would fill a role. Besides looking for gaps, we found some other devices that serve the same purpose and occur frequently in WordNet:

- elided arguments (an IMPRO in the logical form);
- indefinite pronouns (e.g., *something*, *someone*);
- prepositional/adverbial forms containing an IMPRO or an indefinite pronoun (e.g., *give a benediction to*);
- a noun phrase in parentheses (e.g., *to remove (people) from a building*).

The final condition is probably a WN specific device, and was discovered when working on a 10-verb development set, and occurred twice in that set.

Once these arguments are identified, we have a candidate set of roles for the verb. We identify candidate selectional restrictions as described above. Here are a few examples of verbs and their automatically derived roles and restrictions, as computed by our system (here we indicate WordNet entries by their sense index rather than their sense key, since the index is used in the conventional metaphor detection strategy – see below):

bend.v.06:	AGENT/being.n.02 PATIENT/physical_entity.n.01
collect.v.03:	AGENT /person.n.01 PATIENT/object.n.01
drive.v.01:	AGENT/person.n.01 PATIENT/motor_vehicle.n.01
play.v.13:	CAUSE/instrumentality.n.03 EFFECT/music.n.01
walk.v.08:	AGENT/being.n.02 GOAL/location.n.01

The techniques described in this section have been used to provide a set of roles with selectional restrictions for the second IHMC pipeline, described below. The current system takes a list of verbs from a corpus and returns the role names and selectional restrictions for every sense of those words in WordNet.

The transformations described here all equally able to produce preferences for adjectives, as would be needed to detect "*economic muscle*" as a metaphor, which is a form of lexical information not present in any existing database, and the whole process can be applied to any language that possesses a WordNet type lexical resource, and for which we have a capable semantic parser. Hence, these techniques are amenable to being used for detecting metaphorical usage in constructions other than just verb-subject and verb-object, as we do here.

	Pipeline 1 (VerbNet SRs)	Pipeline 2 (WordNet SRs)
TP	24	50
FP	23	37
TN	48	24
FN	37	11
Precision	0.649	0.575
Recall	0.393	0.82
F1	0.49	0.676

Figure 4. Performance comparison between the first pipeline using VerbNet selectional restrictions (SRs) and the second pipeline using WordNet-derived selectional restrictions

7 Conventional Metaphor Detection based on WordNet-Derived Preferences

The preferences and ontology derived from WN definitions greatly improve the mapping between selectional restrictions and WN sense keys. This allows us to replace VN with a new lexical resource that both improves performance, and reduces the complexity of discovering preference violations. In the new pipeline, we can reuse the capabilities developed to extract verbs and their parameters from a sentence. We also reuse the tie-ins to WN that allow us to determine if one WN sense exists within another's hypernym set. It is the selectional restriction lookup that is greatly simplified in the new lexicon, where verbs are mapped directly to WN senses. The conventional metaphor detection is also simplified because the WN senses are included in the responses to the looked up verbs, allowing us to quickly determine if a satisfied verb is conventionalized or is satisfied with conventionalized arguments.

8 Results and Conclusion

Figure 4 shows the results obtained in a metaphor detection task over a small corpus of 122 sentences. Half of these sentences have metaphors and half do not. Of the half that do, approximately half are metaphors about Governance and half are other metaphors. This is not any sort of principled corpus but a seed set chosen to give an initial leverage and in a domain chosen by the sponsor (Governance); the selection and implicit annotation were done by consensus by a large group of twenty or so collaborators. The notion of baseline is irrelevant here, since the choice for every sentence is simply whether it contains a metaphor or not, and could thus be said to be 50% on random assignment of those categories.

From the figures above, it can be seen that the second pipeline does give significant improvement of recall over the first implementation above, even though there is some loss of precision, probably because of the loss of the information in VN. One possibility for integrating a conventional metaphor extraction pipeline like ours with a general metaphor detection pipeline (including, for example, pattern-based methods and top-down recognition from stored Conceptual Metaphors) would be to OR these two pipelines together and to hope to gain the benefits of both, taking anything as a metaphor that was deemed one by either.

However, that is not our aim here: our purpose is only to test the hypothesis that using knowledge derived from existing lexical resources, in combination with some form of the conventionalized metaphor hypothesis, we can achieve good recall performance. On this point we think we have shown the value of the technique.

Acknowledgements

This work was supported in part by the Intelligence Advanced Research Projects Activity (IARPA) via Department of Defense US Army Research Laboratory contract number W911NF-12-C-0020, and NSF grant IIS 1012205. The U.S. Government is authorized to reproduce and distribute reprints for Governmental purposes notwithstanding any copyright annotation thereon. Disclaimer: The views and conclusions contained herein are those of the authors and should not be interpreted as necessarily representing the official policies or endorsements, either expressed or implied, of IARPA, DoD/ARL, or the U.S. Government.

References

James Allen, William de Beaumont, Nate Blaylock, George Ferguson, Jansen Orfan, and Mary Swift. 2011. Acquiring commonsense knowledge for a cognitive agent. In *Proceedings of the AAAI Fall Symposium on Advances in Cognitive Systems* (*ACS 2011*), Arlington, Virginia.

James Allen, Mary Swift, and Will de Beaumont. 2008. Deep semantic analysis of text. In *Proceedings of the 2008 Conference on Semantics in Text Processing* (*STEP '08*), Venice, Italy. pp. 343-354.

Marie-Catherine de Marneffe, Bill MacCartney and Christopher D. Manning. 2006. Generating Typed Dependency Parses from Phrase Structure Parses. In *Proceedings of the 5th International Conference on Language Resources and Evaluation (LREC 2006)*, pp. 449-454.

William B. Dolan. 1995. Metaphor as an emergent property of machine-readable dictionaries. In *Proceedings of the AAAI 1995 Spring Symposium Series: Representation and Acquisition of Lexical Knowledge: Polysemy, Ambiguity and Generativity*, pp. 27–32.

Dan Fass and Yorick Wilks. 1983. Preference semantics, ill-formedness, and metaphor. *American Journal of Computational Linguistics*, 9(3):178–187.

Jenny Rose Finkel, Trond Grenager, and Christopher Manning. 2005. Incorporating Non-local Information into Information Extraction Systems by Gibbs Sampling. In *Proceedings of the 43nd Annual Meeting of the Association for Computational Linguistics (ACL 2005),* pp. 363-370.

David Guthrie, Louise Guthrie, Ben Allison and Yorick Wilks. 2007. Unsupervised Anomaly Detection. In *Proceedings of the 20th international joint conference on Artifical intelligence (IJCAI'07), San Francisco, CA*, pp. 1624-1628.

Karin Kipper, Hoa Trang Dang, and Martha Palmer. 2000. Class-based construction of a verb lexicon. In *Proceedings of the 17th National Conference on Artificial Intelligence*, Austin, Texas. pp. 691-696.

Karin Kipper, Anna Korhonen, Neville Ryant, and Martha Palmer. 2008. A large-scale classification of English verbs. *Language Resources and Evaluation* 42(1):21-40.

Saisuresh Krishnakumaran and Xiaojin Zhu, 2007. Hunting Elusive Metaphors Using Lexical Resources, *Proceedings of the Workshop on Computational Approaches to Figurative Language*, pp. 13-20.

Linlin Li and Caroline Sporleder. 2010. Linguistic Cues for Distinguishing Literal and Non-Literal Usage. In *Proceedings of the 23rd International Conference on Computational Linguistics (COLING 2010)*, Beijing, China, pp. 683-691.

Katia Markert and Nissim Malvina. 2009. Data and Models for Metonymy Resolution. In *Language Resources and Evaluation*, 43(2):123-138.

James Martin. 1990. *A Computational Model of Metaphor Interpretation.* Academic Press.

Zachary J. Mason. 2004. Cormet: A computational, corpus-based conventional metaphor extraction system. *Computational Linguistics*, 30(1):23–44.

Diana McCarthy and John Carrol. 2003. Disambiguating nouns, verbs and adjectives using automatically acquired selectional preferences. *Computational Linguistics.* 29(4): 639-654.

Diana McCarthy, Rob Koeling, Julie Weeds, and John Carroll. 2004. Finding predominant word senses in untagged text. In *Proceedings of the 42nd Annual Meeting on Association for Computational Linguistics* (*ACL '04*), Barcelona, Spain. pp. 280-287.

George Miller. 1995. Wordnet: A lexical database for English. *Communications of the ACM*, 38(11):39-41.

Martha Palmer, Dan Gildea, and Paul Kingsbury. 2005. The Proposition Bank: An Annotated Corpus of Semantic Roles. *Computational Linguistics*, 31(1):71-106.

Wim Peters and Yorick Wilks. 2003. Data-Driven Detection of Figurative Language Use in Electronic Language Resources, *Metaphor and Symbol*, 18(3): 161-174.

Philip Resnik, 1997. Selectional preference and sense disambiguation. In *Proceedings of the ACL SIGLEX Workshop on Tagging Text with Lexical Semantics: Why, What and How?*, Washington, DC, pp. 52-57.

Ekaterina Shutova, Li-ping Sun and Anna Korhonen. 2010. Metaphor Identification Using Verb and Noun Clustering. In *Proceedings of the 23rd International Conference on Computational Linguistics (COLING 2010)*, Beijing, China, pp. 1002-1010.

Yorick Wilks, 1978. Making Preferences More Active. *Artificial Intelligence*, 11(3):197-223.

Cross-Lingual Metaphor Detection Using Common Semantic Features

Yulia Tsvetkov **Elena Mukomel** **Anatole Gershman**
Language Technologies Institute
Carnegie Mellon University
Pittsburgh, PA, 15213, USA
{ytsvetko,helenm,anatoleg}@cs.cmu.edu

Abstract

We present the CSF - Common Semantic Features method for metaphor detection. This method has two distinguishing characteristics: it is cross-lingual and it does not rely on the availability of extensive manually-compiled lexical resources in target languages other than English. A metaphor detecting classifier is trained on English samples and then applied to the target language. The method includes procedures for obtaining semantic features from sentences in the target language. Our experiments with Russian and English sentences show comparable results, supporting our hypothesis that a CSF-based classifier can be applied across languages. We obtain state-of-the-art performance in both languages.

1 Introduction

Metaphors are very powerful pervasive communication tools that help deliver complex concepts and ideas simply and effectively (Lakoff and Johnson, 1980). Automatic detection and interpretation of metaphors is critical for many practical language processing tasks such as information extraction, summarization, opinion mining, and translation. In this paper, we focus on the automatic metaphor detection task. This problem gained much attention in natural language processing research mostly using the detection principles articulated by the Pragglejaz Group (2007). According to these principles, a lexical unit (a word or expression) is used metaphorically if its contextual meaning is different from its "basic contemporary" meaning. To apply this method, we need to be able to determine the basic meaning of a lexical unit and then test if this interpretation makes sense in the current context.

Several approaches to automatic detection of metaphors have been proposed (Gedigian et al., 2006; Krishnakumaran and Zhu, 2007; Shutova et al., 2010), all of which rely on the availability of extensive manually crafted lexical resources such as WordNet, VerbNet, FrameNet, TreeBank, etc. Unfortunately, such resources exist only for a few resource-rich languages such as English. For most other languages, such resources either do not exist or are of a low quality.

To our knowledge this work is the first empirical study of cross-lingual metaphor detection. We present the Common Semantic Features (CSF) approach to metaphor detection in languages without extensive lexical resources. In a target language it requires only a dependency parser and a target-English dictionary. We classify sentences into literal and metaphoric using automatically extracted coarse-grained semantic properties of words such as their propensity to refer to abstract versus concrete concepts, animate entities, artifacts, body parts, etc. These properties serve as features for the key relations in a sentence, which include Subject-Verb-Object (SVO) and Adjective-Noun (AN). A classifier trained on English sentences obtains a 0.78 F-score. The same classifier, trained solely on English sentences, achieves a similar level of performance on sentences from other languages such as Russian; this is the central contribution of this work. An additional important contribution is that in Russian we obtain the necessary semantic features without recourse to sophisticated non-English lexical resources. In this paper, we focus on the sentences where verbs are used metaphorically, leaving Adjective-Noun relations for future work. Based on our examination of over 500 metaphorical sentences in English and Russian collected from general news articles, we estimate that verb-based metaphors constitute about 40-50% of all metaphors.

We present and discuss our experiments with three sets of features: (1) features corresponding to the $lexicographer\ file\ names$ defined in WordNet 3.0 (Fellbaum, 1998), (2) features based on abstractness vs. concreteness computed using Vector Space Models (VSM), and (3) features based on the types of named entities, if present. Our main target language in these experiments has been Russian, but we also present preliminary experiments with Spanish.

The paper is organized as follows: Section 2 contains an overview of the resources we use; Section 3 discusses the methodology; Section 4 presents the experiments; in Section 5, we discuss related work, and we conclude with suggestions for future research in Section 6.

2 Datasets

We use the following English lexical resources to train our model:

TroFi Example Base[1] (Birke and Sarkar, 2007) of 3,737 English sentences from the *Wall Street Journal*. Each sentence contains one of the seed verbs and is marked L by human annotators if the verb is used in a literal sense. Otherwise, the sentence is marked N (non-literal). The model was evaluated on 25 target verbs with manually annotated 1 to 115 sentences per verb. TroFi does not define the basic meanings of these verbs, but provides examples of literal and metaphoric sentences which we use to train and evaluate our metaphor identification method.

WordNet (Fellbaum, 1998) is an English lexical database where each entry contains a set of synonyms (a synset) all representing the same concept. This database is compiled from a set of 45 lexicographer files[2] such as "noun.body" or "verb.cognition" identified by a number from 0 to 44, called $lexicographer\ file\ number$ (henceforth $lexFN$). The $lexFN$ of each synset is contained in the database. We use $lexFNs$ as coarse-grain semantic features of nouns and verbs.

MRC Psycholinguistic Database[3] (Wilson, 1988) is a dictionary containing 150,837 words with up to 26 linguistic and psycholinguistic attributes rated by human subjects in psycholinguistic experiments. It includes 4,295 words rated with degrees of abstractness; the ratings range from 158 (highly abstract) to 670 (highly concrete). We use these words as a seed when we calculate the values of abstractness and concreteness features for nouns and verbs in our training and test sets.

Word Representations via Global Context is a collection of 100,232 words and their vector representations.[4] These representations were extracted from a statistical model embedding both local and global contexts of words (Huang et al., 2012), intended to capture better the semantics of words. We use these vectors to calculate the values of abstractness and concreteness features of a word.

3 Methodology

We treat the metaphor detection problem as a task of binary classification of sentences. A sentence is represented by one or more key relations such as Subject-Verb-Object triples and Adjective-Noun pairs. In this paper, we focus only on the SVO relations and we allow either the S part or the O part to be empty. If all relations representing a sentence are classified literal by our model then the whole sentence is tagged literal. Otherwise, the sentence is tagged metaphoric.

[1]http://www.cs.sfu.ca/ anoop/students/jbirke/

[2]See http://wordnet.princeton.edu/man/lexnames.5WN.html for a full list of lexicographer file names.

[3]http://ota.oucs.ox.ac.uk/headers/1054.xml

[4]http://www.socher.org/index.php/Main/Improving-WordRepresentationsViaGlobalContextAndMultipleWordPrototypes

3.1 Model

We classify an SVO relation $\mathbf{x}$ as literal vs. metaphorical using a logistic regression classifier:

$$p(y \mid \mathbf{x}) \propto \exp \sum_j \lambda_j h_j(y, \mathbf{x}),$$

where $h_j(\cdot)$ are feature values computed for each word in $\mathbf{x}$, λ_j are the corresponding weights, and $y \in \{\texttt{L}, \texttt{M}\}$ refer to our classes: L for literal and M for metaphoric. The parameters λ_j are learned during training.

3.2 Features

An SVO relation is a concatenation of features for the S, V, and O parts. The S and O parts contain three types of features: (1) semantic categories of a word, (2) degree of abstractness of a word, and (3) types of named entities. The V part contains only the first two types of features.

Semantic categories are features corresponding to the WordNet $lexFNs$, introduced in Section 2. Since S and O are assumed to be nouns,[5] each has 26 semantic category features corresponding to the $lexFNs$ for nouns (3 through 28). These categories include *noun.animal, noun.artefact, noun.body, noun.cognition, noun.food, noun.location*, etc. The V part has 15 semantic category features corresponding to lexical ids for verbs (29 through 43), for example, *verb.motion* and *verb.cognition*. A lexical item can belong to several synsets with different $lexFNs$. For example, the word "head" when used as a noun participates in 33 synsets, 3 of which have $lexFN$ 08 (*noun.body*). The value of the feature corresponding to this $lexFN$ is $3/33 = 0.09$.

For a non-English word, we first obtain its most common translations to English and then select all corresponding English WordNet synsets. For example, when Russian word 'голова' is translated as *'head'* and *'brain'*, we select all the synsets for the nouns *head* and *brain*. There are 38 such synsets (33 for *head* and 5 for *brain*). Four of these synsets have $lexFN$ 08 (*noun.body*). Therefore, the value of the feature corresponding to this $lexFN$ is $4/38 = 0.10$. This dictionary-based mapping of non-English words into WN synsets is rather coarse. A more discriminating approach may improve the overall performance. In addition, WN synsets may not always capture all the meanings of non-English words. For example, Russian word 'нога' refers to both the *'foot'* and the *'leg'*. WN has synsets for *foot, leg* and *extremity*, but not for *lower extremity*.

Degree of abstractness According to Turney et al. (2011), "Abstract words refer to ideas and concepts that are distant from immediate perception, such as economics, calculating and disputable." Concrete words refer to physical objects and actions. Words with multiple senses can refer to both concrete and abstract concepts. Evidence from several languages suggests that concrete verbs tend to have concrete subjects and objects. If either the subject or an object of a concrete verb is abstract, then the verb is typically used in a figurative sense, indicating the presence of a metaphor. For example, when we hear that "an idea was born", we know that the word "born" is used figuratively. This observation motivates our decision to include the degree of abstractness in our feature set.

To calculate the degree of abstractness of English lexical items we use the vector space representations of words computed by Huang et al. (2012) and a separate supervised logistic regression classifier trained on a set of abstract and concrete words from the MRC dataset. Each value in a word's vector is a feature, thus, semantically similar words have similar feature values. Degrees of abstractness are posterior probabilities of the classifier predictions.

For non-English words, we use the following procedure. Suppose word w has n English translations whose degrees of abstractness are $a_1, a_2, \ldots a_n$ in decreasing order. If the majority is deemed abstract then $ABSTRACT(w) = a_1$, otherwise $ABSTRACT(w) = a_n$. This heuristic prefers the extreme interpretations, and is based on an observation that translations tend to be skewed to one side or the other of "abstractness". Our results may improve if we map non-English words more precisely into the most contextually-appropriate English senses.

Named entities (NE) is an additional category of features instrumental in metaphor identification. Specifically, we would like to distinguish whether an action (a verb in SVO) is performed by a human,

[5]We currently exclude pronouns from the relations that we learn.

an organization or a geographical entity. These distinctions are often needed to detect metonymy, as in "the White House said". Often, these entities are mentioned by their names which are not found in common dictionaries. Fortunately, there are many named entity recognizers (NER) for all major languages. In addition, Shah et al. (2010) showed that named entities tend to survive popular machine translation engines and can be relatively reliably detected even without a native NER. Based on these observations, we decided to include three boolean features corresponding to these NE categories: person, organization, and location.

4 Experiments

We train two classifiers: the first to calculate the degree of abstractness of a given word and the second to classify an SVO relation as metaphoric or literal. Both are logistic regression classifiers trained with the `creg` regression modeling framework.[6] To minimize the number of free parameters in our model we use ℓ_1 regularization.

4.1 Measuring abstractness

To train the abstractness classifier, we normalize abstractness scores of nouns from the MRC dataset to probabilities, and select 1,225 most abstract and 1,225 most concrete words. From these words, we set aside 25 randomly selected samples from each category for testing. We obtain the vector space representations of the remaining 1,400 samples and use the dimensions of these representations as features. We train the abstractness classifier on the 1,400 labeled samples and test it on the 50 samples that were set aside, obtaining 76% accuracy. The degree of abstractness of a word is the posterior probability produced by the abstractness classifier.

4.2 Metaphor detection

We train the metaphor classifier using labeled English SVO relations. To obtain these relations, we use the Turbo parser (Martins et al., 2010) to parse 1,592 literal and 1,609 metaphorical manually annotated sentences from the TroFi Example Base and extract 1,660 sentences that have SVO relations that contain annotated verbs: 696 literal and 964 metaphorical training instances. For example, the verb *flourish* is used literally in *"Methane-making bacteria flourish in the stomach"* and metaphorically in *"Economies flourish in free markets"*. From the first sentence we extract SVO relation `<bacteria, flourish, NIL>`, and `<economies, flourish, NIL>` from the second. We then build feature vectors, using feature categories described in Section 3.

We train several versions of the metaphor classifier for each feature category and for their combinations. The feature categories are designated as follows:

- WN - Semantic categories based on WordNet $lexFNs$
- VSM - Degree of abstractness based on word vectors
- NE - Named Entity categories

We evaluate the metaphor classifiers using 10-fold cross validation. The results are listed in Table 1.

Feature categories	Accuracy
WN	63.7%
VSM	64.1%
WN+VSM	67.7%
WN+NE	64.5%
WN+VSM+NE	**69.0%**

Table 1: 10-fold cross validation results of the metaphor classifier.

Our results are comparable to the accuracy of 64.9% reported by Birke and Sarkar (2007) on the TroFi dataset. The combination of all feature categories significantly improves over this baseline.

4.2.1 English metaphor detection

We compute precision, recall and F-score on a test set of 98 English sentences. This test set consists of 50 literal and 48 metaphorical sentences, where each metaphoric sentence contains a verb used in a figurative sense. The test sentences were selected from general news articles by independent collectors. Table 2 shows the results.

In this experiment, the WN group of features contributes the most. The addition of NE, while not improving the overall F-score, helps to reduce false positives and better balance precision and recall. The VSM features are considerably weaker perhaps

[6]https://github.com/redpony/creg

Feature categories	Precision	Recall	F-score
WN	0.75	0.81	0.78
VSM	0.57	0.71	0.63
WN+VSM	0.66	0.90	0.76
WN+NE	0.78	0.79	**0.78**
WN+VSM+NE	0.68	0.71	0.69

Table 2: Evaluation of the metaphor classifier on the test set of 50 literal and 48 metaphoric English sentences from news articles.

because we used single model vector space representations where each word uses only one vector that combines all its senses.

4.2.2 Russian metaphor detection

In a cross-lingual experiment, we evaluate our algorithm on a set of 140 Russian sentences: 62 literal and 78 metaphoric, selected from general news articles by two independent collectors. As in English, each metaphoric sentence contains a verb used in a figurative sense. We used the AOT parser[7] to obtain the SVO relations and the Babylon dictionary[8] to obtain English translations of individual words. The example sentence in Figure 1 contains one SVO relation with missing O part. We show the set of features and their values that were extracted from words in this relation.

The results of the Russian test set, listed in Table 3, are similar to the English results, supporting our hypothesis that a semantic classifier can work across languages. As in the previous experiment, the WN features are the most effective and the NE features contribute to improved precision.

Feature categories	Precision	Recall	F-score
WN	0.74	0.76	0.75
VSM	0.66	0.73	0.69
WN+VSM	0.70	0.73	0.71
WN+NE	0.82	0.71	**0.76**
WN+VSM+NE	0.74	0.72	0.73

Table 3: Evaluation of the metaphor classifier on the test set of 62 literal and 78 metaphoric Russian sentences from news articles.

While we did not conduct a full-scale experiment with Spanish, we ran a pilot using 51 sentences: 24 literal and 27 metaphoric. We obtained the F-score of 0.66 for the WN+VSM combination. We take it as a positive sign and will conduct more experiments.

5 Related work

Our work builds on the research of Birke and Sarkar (2007) who used an active learning approach to create an annotated corpus of sentences with literal and figurative senses of 50 common English verbs. The result was the TroFi Example Base set of 3,737 labeled sentences, which was used by the authors to train several classifiers. These algorithms were tested on sentences containing 25 English verbs not included in the original set. The authors report F-scores around 64.9%. We used this dataset for training and evaluation, and Birke and Sarkar's (2007) results as a baseline.

In a more recent work, Turney et al. (2011) suggested that the degree of abstractness of a word's context is correlated with the likelihood that the word is used metaphorically. To compute the abstractness of a word, the authors use a variation of Turney and Littman's (2003) algorithm comparing the word to twenty typically abstract words and twenty typically concrete words. Latent Semantic Analysis (Deerwester et al., 1990) is used to measure semantic similarity between each pair of words. A feature vector is generated for each word and a logistic regression classifier is used. The result is an average F-score of 63.9% on the TroFi dataset,[9] compared to Birke and Sarkar's (2007) 64.9%. In another experiment on 100 adjective-noun phrases labeled as literal or non-literal, according to the sense of the adjective, this algorithm obtains an average accuracy of 79%. While we obtain comparable results, our work extends this method in several important directions. First, we show how to apply a metaphor classifier across languages. Second, we extend our feature set beyond abstractness criteria. Finally, we propose an alternative technique to measure degrees of abstractness.

[7] www.aot.ru

[8] www.babylon.com

[9] Turney et al. (2011) report on two experimental setups with TroFi, our setup is closer to their first experiment.

Общество зреет десятилетиями .
'Society ripens over decades'

SVO = <Общество, зреет, NIL>

	Subject		Verb	
WN	noun.group noun.state noun.possession noun.location	0.54 0.23 0.15 0.08	verb.change verb.body verb.communication	0.75 0.125 0.125
VSM	Abstractness	0.87	Abstractness	0.93

Figure 1: Features extracted for a Russian test sentence classified as metaphoric by our model.

6 Conclusions and future work

We presented CSF – an approach to metaphor detection based on semantic rather than lexical features. We described our experiments with an initial set of fairly coarse-grained features and showed how these features can be obtained in languages that lack extensive lexical resources. Semantic, as opposed to lexical features, are common to all languages which allows a classifier trained to detect metaphors in one language to be successfully applied to sentences in another language. Our results suggest that metaphors can be detected on a conceptual level, independently of whether they are expressed in Russian or English, supporting Lakoff and Johnson's (1980) claim that metaphors are parts of a pervasive conceptual system.

Our current work has been limited to the detection of figurative SVO relations, which account for about half of all metaphors in English and Russian. Other languages such as Farsi have a greater proportion of metaphors based on figurative use of adjectives and nouns. We plan to include more relations and expand our set of semantic features as part of the future research.

Acknowledgments

We are grateful to Chris Dyer for his invaluable advice. We are also grateful to the three anonymous reviewers for their constructive suggestions. Supported by the Intelligence Advanced Research Projects Activity (IARPA) via Department of Defense US Army Research Laboratory contract number W911NF-12-C-0020. The U.S. Government is authorized to reproduce and distribute reprints for Governmental purposes notwithstanding any copyright annotation thereon. Disclaimer: The views and conclusions contained herein are those of the authors and should not be interpreted as necessarily representing the official policies or endorsements, either expressed or implied, of IARPA, DoD/ARL, or the U.S. Government.

References

Julia Birke and Anoop Sarkar. 2007. Active learning for the identification of nonliteral language. In *Proceedings of the Workshop on Computational Approaches to Figurative Language*, FigLanguages '07, pages 21–28.

Scott C. Deerwester, Susan T. Dumais, Thomas K. Landauer, George W. Furnas, and Richard A. Harshman. 1990. Indexing by latent semantic analysis. *Journal of the American Society of Information Science*, 41(6):391–407.

Christiane Fellbaum, editor. 1998. *WordNet: An Electronic Lexical Database*. Language, Speech and Communication. MIT Press.

Matt Gedigian, John Bryant, Srini Narayanan, and Branimir Ciric. 2006. Catching metaphors. In *Proceedings of the 3rd Workshop on Scalable Natural Language Understanding*, pages 41–48.

Pragglejaz Group. 2007. MIP: A method for identifying metaphorically used words in discourse. *Metaphor and Symbol*, 22(1):1–39.

Eric H. Huang, Richard Socher, Christopher D. Manning, and Andrew Y. Ng. 2012. Improving word representations via global context and multiple word prototypes. In *Annual Meeting of the Association for Computational Linguistics*, ACL 2012.

Saisuresh Krishnakumaran and Xiaojin Zhu. 2007. Hunting elusive metaphors using lexical resources. In *Proceedings of the Workshop on Computational approaches to Figurative Language*, pages 13–20.

George Lakoff and Mark Johnson. 1980. Conceptual metaphor in everyday language. *The Journal of Philosophy*, pages 453–486.

André F. T. Martins, Noah A. Smith, Eric P. Xing, Pedro M. Q. Aguiar, and Mário A. T. Figueiredo. 2010. Turbo parsers: dependency parsing by approximate variational inference. In *Proceedings of the 2010 Conference on Empirical Methods in Natural Language Processing*, EMNLP '10, pages 34–44.

Rushin Shah, Bo Lin, Anatole Gershman, and Robert Frederking. 2010. SYNERGY: a named entity recognition system for resource-scarce languages such as Swahili using online machine translation. In *Proceedings of the Second Workshop on African Language Technology*, AfLaT 2010, pages 21–26.

Ekaterina Shutova, Lin Sun, and Anna Korhonen. 2010. Metaphor identification using verb and noun clustering. In *Proceedings of the 23rd International Conference on Computational Linguistics*, pages 1002–1010.

Peter D. Turney and Michael L. Littman. 2003. Measuring praise and criticism: Inference of semantic orientation from association. *ACM Transactions on Information and System Security*, 21(4):315–346.

Peter D. Turney, Yair Neuman, Dan Assaf, and Yohai Cohen. 2011. Literal and metaphorical sense identification through concrete and abstract context. In *Proceedings of the Conference on Empirical Methods in Natural Language Processing*, EMNLP '11, pages 680–690.

Michael Wilson. 1988. MRC Psycholinguistic Database: Machine-usable dictionary, version 2.00. *Behavior Research Methods, Instruments, & Computers*, 20(1):6–10.

Identifying Metaphorical Word Use with Tree Kernels

Dirk Hovy[1] **Shashank Srivastava**[2] **Sujay Kumar Jauhar**[2] **Mrinmaya Sachan**[2]
Kartik Goyal[2] **Huiying Li**[2] **Whitney Sanders**[2] **Eduard Hovy**[2]
(1) ISI, University of Southern California, Marina del Rey
(2) LTI, Carnegie Mellon University, Pittsburgh
dirkh@isi.edu, {shashans,sjauhar,mrinmays,kartikgo,huiyingl,wsanders,hovy}@cs.cmu.edu

Abstract

A metaphor is a figure of speech that refers to one concept in terms of another, as in "He is such a *sweet* person". Metaphors are ubiquitous and they present NLP with a range of challenges for WSD, IE, etc. Identifying metaphors is thus an important step in language understanding. However, since almost any word can serve as a metaphor, they are impossible to list. To identify metaphorical use, we assume that it results in unusual semantic patterns between the metaphor and its dependencies. To identify these cases, we use SVMs with tree-kernels on a balanced corpus of 3872 instances, created by bootstrapping from available metaphor lists.[1] We outperform two baselines, a sequential and a vector-based approach, and achieve an F1-score of 0.75.

1 Introduction

A metaphor is a figure of speech used to transfer qualities of one concept to another, as in "He is such a sweet person". Here, the qualities of "sweet" (the *source*) are transferred to a person (the *target*). Traditionally, linguistics has modeled metaphors as a mapping from one domain to another (Lakoff and Johnson, 1980).

Metaphors are ubiquitous in normal language and present NLP with a range of challenges. First, due to their very nature, they cannot be interpreted at face value, with consequences for WSD, IE, etc. Second, metaphors are very productive constructions, and almost any word can be used metaphorically (e.g., "This is the **Donald Trump** of sandwiches."). This property makes them impossible to pre-define or list. Third, repeated use of a metaphor eventually solidifies it into a fixed expression with the metaphorical meaning now accepted as just another sense, no longer recognized as metaphorical at all. This gradient makes it hard to determine a boundary between literal and metaphorical use of some expressions. Identifying metaphors is thus a difficult but important step in language understanding.[2]

Since many words can be productively used as new metaphors, approaches that try to identify them based on lexical features alone are bound to be unsuccessful. Some approaches have therefore suggested considering distributional properties and "abstractness" of the phrase (Turney et al., 2011). This nicely captures the contextual nature of metaphors, but their ubiquity makes it impossible to find truly "clean" data to learn the separate distributions of metaphorical and literal use for each word. Other approaches have used pre-defined mappings from a source to a target domain, as in "X is like Y", e.g., "emotions are like temperature" (Mason, 2004). These approaches tend to do well on the defined mappings, but they do not generalize to new, creative metaphors. It is doubtful that it is feasible to list all possible mappings, so these approaches remain brittle.

In contrast, we do not assume any predefined mappings. We hypothesize instead that if we interpreted every word literally, metaphors will manifest themselves as unusual semantic compositions. Since these compositions most frequently occur

[1] Available at http://www.edvisees.cs.cmu.edu/metaphordata.tar.gz

[2] Shutova (2010) distinguishes between metaphor *identification* (which she calls recognition) and *interpretation*. We are solely concerned with the former.

in certain syntactic relations, they are usually considered semantic preference violations; e.g., in the metaphorical "You will have to **eat** your words", the food-related verb heads a noun of communication. In contrast, with the literal sense of "eat" in "You will have to **eat** your peas", it heads a food noun. This intuition is the basis of the approaches in (Iverson and Helmreich, 1991; Krishnakumaran and Zhu, 2007; Baumer et al., 2010; Turney et al., 2011).[3] We generalize this intuition beyond preference selections of verbs and relational nouns.

Given enough labeled examples of a word, we expect to find distinctive differences in the compositional behavior of its literal and metaphorical uses in certain preferred syntactic relationships. *If we can learn to detect such differences/anomalies, we can reliably identify metaphors.* Since we expect these patterns in levels other than the lexical level, the approach expands well to creative metaphors.

The observation that the anomaly tends to occur between syntactically related words makes dependency tree kernels a natural fit for the problem. Tree kernels have been successfully applied to a wide range of NLP tasks that involve (syntactic) relations (Culotta and Sorensen, 2004; Moschitti, 2006; Qian et al., 2008; Giuliano et al., 2009; Mirroshandel et al., 2011).

Our contributions in this paper are:

- we annotate and release a corpus of 3872 instances for supervised metaphor classification
- we are the first to use tree kernels for metaphor identification
- our approach achieves an F1-score of 0.75, the best score of of all systems tested.

2 Data

2.1 Annotation

We downloaded a list of 329 metaphor examples from the web[4]. For each expression, we extracted sentences from the Brown corpus that contained the seed (see Figure 1 for an example). To decide whether a particular instance is used metaphorically, we set up an annotation task on Amazon Mechanical Turk (AMT).

Annotators were asked to decide whether a highlighted expression in a sentence was used metaphorically or not (see Figure 2 for a screenshot). They were prompted to think about whether the expression was used in its original meaning.[5] In some cases, it is not clear whether an expression is used metaphorically or not (usually in short sentences such as "That's sweet"), so annotators could state that it was not possible to decide. We paid $0.09 for each set of 10 instances.

Each instance was annotated by 7 annotators. Instances where the annotators agreed that it was impossible to tell whether it is a metaphor or not were discarded. Inter-annotator agreement was 0.57, indicating a difficult task. In order to get the label for each instance, we weighted the annotator's answers using MACE (Hovy et al., 2013), an implementation of an unsupervised item-response model. This weighted voting produces more reliable estimates than simple majority voting, since it is capable of sorting out unreliable annotators. The final corpus consisted of 3872 instances, 1749 of them labeled as metaphors.

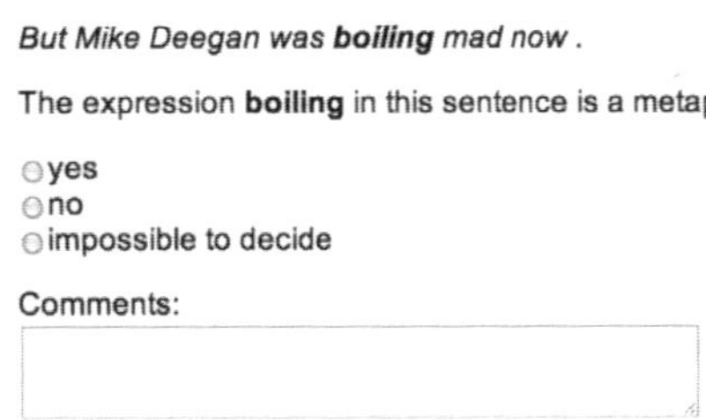

Figure 2: Screenshot of the annotation interface on Amazon's Mechanical Turk

We divided the data into training, dev, and test sets, using a 80-10-10 split. All results reported here were obtained on the test set. Tuning and development was only carried out on the dev set.

2.2 Vector Representation of Words

The same word may occur in a literal and a metaphorical usage. Lexical information alone is

[3] A similar assumption can be used to detect the literal/non-literal uses of idioms (Fazly et al., 2009).

[4] http://www.metaphorlist.com and http://www.macmillandictionaryblog.com

[5] While this is somewhat imprecise and not always easy to decide, it proved to be a viable strategy for untrained annotators.

*A **bright** idea.*

“ Peter is the **bright** , sympathetic guy when you ’re doing a deal , ” says one agent .	*yes*
Below he could see the **bright** torches lighting the riverbank .	*no*
Her **bright** eyes were twinkling .	*yes*
Washed , they came out surprisingly clear and **bright** .	*no*

Figure 1: Examples of a metaphor seed, the matching Brown sentences, and their annotations

thus probably not very helpful. However, we would like to capture semantic aspects of the word and represent it in an expressive way. We use the existing vector representation SENNA (Collobert et al., 2011) which is derived from contextual similarity. In it, semantically similar words are represented by similar vectors, without us having to define similarity or looking at the word itself. In initial tests, these vectors performed better than binary vectors straightforwardly derived from features of the word in context.

2.3 Constructing Trees

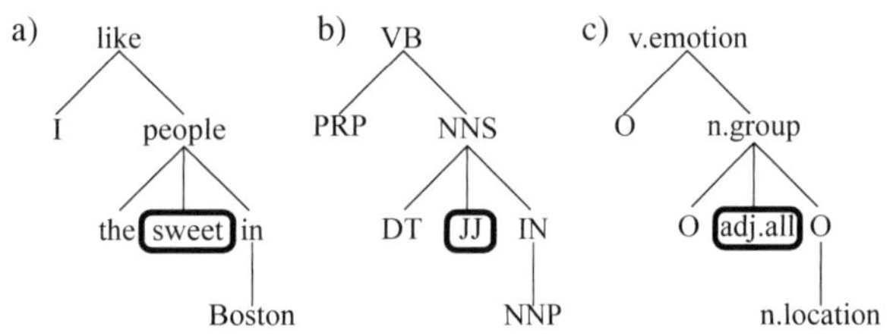

Figure 3: Graphic demonstration of our approach. a) dependency tree over words, with node of interest labeled. b) as POS representation. c) as supersense representation

The intuition behind our approach is that metaphorical use differs from literal use in certain syntactic relations. For example, the only difference between the two sentences “I like the sweet people in Boston” and “I like the sweet pies in Boston” is the head of “sweet”. Our assumption is that—given enough examples—certain patterns emerge (e.g., that “sweet” in combination with food nouns is literal, but is metaphorical if governed by a noun denoting people).

We assume that these patterns occur on different levels, and mainly between syntactically related words. We thus need a data representation to capture these patterns. We borrow its structure from dependency trees, and the different levels from various annotations. We parse the input sentence with the FANSE parser (Tratz and Hovy, 2011)[6]. It provides the dependency structure, POS tags, and other information.

To construct the different tree representations, we replace each node in the tree with its word, lemma, POS tag, dependency label, or supersense (the WordNet lexicographer name of the word’s first sense (Fellbaum, 1998)), and mark the word in question with a special node. See Figure 3 for a graphical representation. These trees are used *in addition* to the vectors.

This approach is similar to the ones described in (Moschitti et al., 2006; Qian et al., 2008; Hovy et al., 2012).

2.4 Classification Models

A tree kernel is simply a similarity matrix over tree instances. It computes the similarity between two trees T_1, T_2 based on the number of shared subtrees.

We want to make use of the information encoded in the different tree representations during classification, i.e., a forest of tree kernels. We thus combine the contributions of the individual tree representation kernels via addition. We use kernels over the lemma, POS tag, and supersense tree representations, the combination which performed best on the dev set in terms of accuracy.

We use the SVMlight TK implementation by Moschitti (2006).[7] We left most parameters set to default values, but tuned the weight of the contribution of the trees and the cost factor on the dev set. We set the multiplicative constant for the trees to 2.0, and the cost factor for errors on positive examples to 1.7.

[6]http://www.isi.edu/publications/licensed-sw/fanseparser/index.html

[7]http://disi.unitn.it/moschitti/Tree-Kernel.htm

If we assume any word can be used metaphorically, we ultimately want to label every word in a sentence, so we also evaluate a sequential model, in this case a CRF. We use CRFsuite (Okazaki, 2007)[8] to implement the CRF, and run it with averaged perceptron. While the CRF produces labels for *every* word, we only evaluate on the words that were annotated in our corpus (to make it maximally comparable), and use the same representations (lemma, POS and SST) of the word and its parent as features as we did for the SVM. Training method and feature selection were again tuned on the dev set to maximize accuracy.

3 Experiments

system	acc	P	R	F1
BL_{all}	0.49	0.49	1.0	0.66
$BL_{most\ freq.\ class}$	0.70	0.66	0.65	0.65
CRF	0.69*	**0.74***	0.50	0.59
$SVM_{vector-only}$	0.70*	0.63*	0.80	0.71
SVM_{+tree}	**0.75***	0.70*	**0.80**	**0.75***

Table 1: Accuracy, precision, recall, and F1 for various systems on the held-out test set. Values significantly better than baseline at $p < .02$ are marked * (two-tailed t-test).

We compare the performance of two baselines, the CRF model, vanilla SVM, and SVM with tree kernels and report accuracy, precision, recall, and F1 (Table 1).

The first baseline (BL_{all}) labels every instance as metaphor. Its accuracy and precision reflect the metaphor ratio in the data, and it naturally achieves perfect recall. This is a rather indiscriminate approach and not very viable in practice, so we also apply a more realistic baseline, labeling each word with the class it received most often in the training data ($BL_{most\ freq.\ class}$). This is essentially like assuming that every word has a default class. Accuracy and precision for this baseline are much better, although recall naturally suffers.

The CRF improves in terms of accuracy and precision, but lacks the high recall the baseline has, resulting in a lower F1-score. It does yield the highest precision of all models, though. So while not capturing every metaphor in the data, it is usually correct if it does label a word as metaphor.

SVMlight allows us to evaluate the performance of a classification using *only* the vector representation ($SVM_{vector-only}$). This model achieves better accuracy and recall than the CRF, but is less precise. Accuracy is the same as for the most-frequent-class baseline, indicating that the vector-based SVM learns to associate a class with each lexical item. Once we add the tree kernels to the vector (SVM_{+tree}), we see considerable gains in accuracy and precision. This confirms our hypothesis that metaphors are not only a lexical phenomenon, but also a product of the context a word is used in. The contextual interplay with their dependencies creates patterns that can be exploited with tree kernels. We note that the SVM with tree kernels is the only system whose F1 significantly improves over the baseline (at $p < .02$).

Testing with one tree representation at a time, we found the various representations differ in terms of informativeness. Lemma, POS, and supersense performed better than lexemes or dependency labels (when evaluated on the dev set) and were thus used in the reported system. Combining more than one representation in the same tree to form compound leaves (e.g. lemma+POS, such as "man-NN") performed worse in all combinations tested. We omit further details here, since the combinatorics of these tests are large and yield only little insight.

Overall, our results are similar to comparable methods on balanced corpora, and we encourage the evaluation of other methods on our data set.

4 Related Work

There is plenty of research into metaphors. While many are mainly interested in their general properties (Shutova, 2010; Nayak, 2011), we focus on the ones that evaluate their results empirically.

Gedigian et al. (2006) use a similar approach to identify metaphors, but focus on frames. Their corpus is with about 900 instances relatively small. They improve over the majority baseline, but only report accuracy. Both their result and the baseline are in the 90s, which might be due to the high number of metaphors (about 90%). We use a larger,

[8]http://www.chokkan.org/software/crfsuite/

more balanced data set. Since accuracy can be uninformative in cases of unbalanced data sets, we also report precision, recall, and F1.

Krishnakumaran and Zhu (2007) also use semantic relations between syntactic dependencies as basis for their classification. They do not aim to distinguish literal and metaphorical use, but try to differentiate various types of metaphors. They use a corpus of about 1700 sentences containing different metaphors, and report a precision of 0.70, recall of 0.61 (F1 = 0.65), and accuracy of 0.58.

Birke and Sarkar (2006) and Birke and Sarkar (2007) present unsupervised and active learning approaches to classifying metaphorical and literal expressions, reporting F1 scores of 0.54 and 0.65, outperforming baseline approaches. Unfortunately, as they note themselves, their data set is "not large enough to [...] support learning using a supervised learning method" (Birke and Sarkar, 2007, 22), which prevents a direct comparison.

Similarly to our corpus construction, (Shutova et al., 2010) use bootstrapping from a small seed set. They use an unsupervised clustering approach to identify metaphors and report a precision of 0.79, beating the baseline system by a wide margin. Due to the focus on corpus construction, they cannot provide recall or F1. Their approach considers only pairs of a single verbs and nouns, while we allow for any syntactic combination.

Tree kernels have been applied to a wide variety of NLP tasks (Culotta and Sorensen, 2004; Moschitti et al., 2006; Qian et al., 2008; Hovy et al., 2012). They are specifically adept in capturing long-range syntactic relationships. In our case, we use them to detect anomalies in syntactic relations.

5 Conclusion

Under the hypothesis that the metaphorical use of a word creates unusual patterns with its dependencies, we presented the first tree-kernel based approach to metaphor identification. Syntactic dependencies allow us to capture those patterns at different levels of representations and identify metaphorical use more reliably than non-kernel methods. We outperform two baselines, a sequential model, and purely vector-based SVM approaches, and reach an F1 of 0.75. Our corpus is available for download at `http://www.edvisees.cs.cmu.edu/metaphordata.tar.gz` and we encourage the research community to evaluate other methods on it.

Acknowledgements

The authors would like to thank the reviewers for helping us clarify several points and giving constructive input that helped to improve the quality of this paper. This work was (in part) supported by the Intelligence Advanced Research Projects Activity (IARPA) via Department of Defense US Army Research Laboratory contract number W911NF-12-C-0025. The U.S. Government is authorized to reproduce and distribute reprints for Governmental purposes notwithstanding any copyright annotation thereon. Disclaimer: The views and conclusions contained herein are those of the authors and should not be interpreted as necessarily representing the official policies or endorsements, either expressed or implied, of IARPA, DoD/ARL, or the U.S. Government.

References

Eric P.S. Baumer, James P. White, and Bill Tomlinson. 2010. Comparing semantic role labeling with typed dependency parsing in computational metaphor identification. In *Proceedings of the NAACL HLT 2010 Second Workshop on Computational Approaches to Linguistic Creativity*, pages 14–22. Association for Computational Linguistics.

Julia Birke and Anoop Sarkar. 2006. A clustering approach for the nearly unsupervised recognition of nonliteral language. In *Proceedings of EACL*, volume 6, pages 329–336.

Julia Birke and Anoop Sarkar. 2007. Active learning for the identification of nonliteral language. In *Proceedings of the Workshop on Computational Approaches to Figurative Language*, pages 21–28. Association for Computational Linguistics.

Ronan Collobert, Jason Weston, Léon Bottou, Michael Karlen, Koray Kavukcuoglu, and Pavel Kuksa. 2011. Natural language processing (almost) from scratch. *Journal of Machine Learning Research*, 12:2493–2537.

Aron Culotta and Jeffrey Sorensen. 2004. Dependency tree kernels for relation extraction. In *Proceedings of the 42nd Annual Meeting on Association for Computational Linguistics*, page 423. Association for Computational Linguistics.

Afsaneh Fazly, Paul Cook, and Suzanne Stevenson. 2009. Unsupervised type and token identification of idiomatic expressions. *Computational Linguistics*, 35(1):61–103.

Christiane Fellbaum. 1998. *WordNet: an electronic lexical database*. MIT Press USA.

Matt Gedigian, John Bryant, Srini Narayanan, and Branimir Ciric. 2006. Catching metaphors. In *Proceedings of the 3rd Workshop on Scalable Natural Language Understanding*, pages 41–48.

Claudio Giuliano, Alfio Massimiliano Gliozzo, and Carlo Strapparava. 2009. Kernel methods for minimally supervised wsd. *Computational Linguistics*, 35(4).

Dirk Hovy, James Fan, Alfio Gliozzo, Siddharth Patwardhan, and Christopher Welty. 2012. When Did that Happen? — Linking Events and Relations to Timestamps. In *Proceedings of EACL*.

Dirk Hovy, Taylor Berg-Kirkpatrick, Ashish Vaswani, and Eduard Hovy. 2013. Learning Whom to trust with MACE. In *Proceedings of NAACL HLT*.

Eric Iverson and Stephen Helmreich. 1991. Non-literal word sense identification through semantic network path schemata. In *Proceedings of the 29th annual meeting on Association for Computational Linguistics*, pages 343–344. Association for Computational Linguistics.

Saishuresh Krishnakumaran and Xiaojian Zhu. 2007. Hunting elusive metaphors using lexical resources. In *Proceedings of the Workshop on Computational approaches to Figurative Language*, pages 13–20. Association for Computational Linguistics.

George Lakoff and Mark Johnson. 1980. *Metaphors we live by*, volume 111. University of Chicago Press.

Zachary J. Mason. 2004. CorMet: a computational, corpus-based conventional metaphor extraction system. *Computational Linguistics*, 30(1):23–44.

Seyed A. Mirroshandel, Mahdy Khayyamian, and Gholamreza Ghassem-Sani. 2011. Syntactic tree kernels for event-time temporal relation learning. *Human Language Technology. Challenges for Computer Science and Linguistics*, pages 213–223.

Alessandro Moschitti, Daniele Pighin, and Roberto Basili. 2006. Tree kernel engineering for proposition re-ranking. *MLG 2006*, page 165.

Alessandro Moschitti. 2006. Making Tree Kernels Practical for Natural Language Learning. In *In Proceedings of the 11th Conference of the European Chapter of the Association for Computational Linguistics*.

Sushobhan Nayak. 2011. Towards a grounded model for ontological metaphors. In *Student Research Workshop*, pages 115–120.

Naoaki Okazaki. 2007. CRFsuite: a fast implementation of Conditional Random Fields (CRFs).

Longhua Qian, Guodong Zhou, Fang Kong, Qiaoming Zhu, and Peide Qian. 2008. Exploiting constituent dependencies for tree kernel-based semantic relation extraction. In *Proceedings of the 22nd International Conference on Computational Linguistics-Volume 1*, pages 697–704. Association for Computational Linguistics.

Ekaterina Shutova, Lin Sun, and Anna Korhonen. 2010. Metaphor identification using verb and noun clustering. In *Proceedings of the 23rd International Conference on Computational Linguistics*, pages 1002–1010. Association for Computational Linguistics.

Ekaterina Shutova. 2010. Models of metaphor in nlp. In *Proceedings of the 48th Annual Meeting of the Association for Computational Linguistics*, pages 688–697. Association for Computational Linguistics.

Stephen Tratz and Eduard Hovy. 2011. A fast, accurate, non-projective, semantically-enriched parser. In *Proceedings of the Conference on Empirical Methods in Natural Language Processing*, pages 1257–1268. Association for Computational Linguistics.

Peter D. Turney, Yair Neuman, Dan Assaf, and Yohai Cohen. 2011. Literal and metaphorical sense identification through concrete and abstract context. In *Proceedings of the 2011 Conference on the Empirical Methods in Natural Language Processing*, pages 680–690.

Automatic Extraction of Linguistic Metaphor with LDA Topic Modeling

Ilana Heintz*, Ryan Gabbard*, Mahesh Srinivasan+, *, David Barner+, Donald S. Black*, Marjorie Freedman*, Ralph Weischedel*

* Raytheon BBN Technologies
10 Moulton St,
Cambridge MA 02139

{iheintz, rgabbard, mfreedman, dblack, rweischedel}@bbn.com

+University of California, San Diego
5336 McGill Hall,
9500 Gilman Drive
La Jolla, CA 92093-0109

barner@ucsd.edu, mahesh.srinivasan@gmail.com

Abstract

We aim to investigate cross-cultural patterns of thought through cross-linguistic investigation of the use of metaphor. As a first step, we produce a system for locating instances of metaphor in English and Spanish text. In contrast to previous work which relies on resources like syntactic parsing and WordNet, our system is based on LDA topic modeling, enabling its application even to low-resource languages, and requires no labeled data. We achieve an F-score of 59% for English.

1 Introduction

Patterns in the use of metaphors can provide a great deal of insight into a culture. Cultural differences expressed linguistically as metaphor can play a role in matters as complex and important as diplomatic relations. For instance, Thornborrow (1993) discusses the different metaphors that are used in the context of *security* in French and British coverage of two major post-cold-war summit meetings. Example metaphors such as "the cornerstone of the new security structure," "structures for defence and security cooperation," and "the emerging shape of Europe," exemplify the English use of the **source concept** *structure* in describing the **target concept** of *security*. In contrast, the metaphors "des règles de sécurité nouvelles (new rules of security)", "une révision fondamentale des dispositions de sécurité (a fundamental revision of security provisions)", and "un système de sécurité européen (a system of European security)" exemplify the French use of the more abstract source concept *system* to describe the same target concept. As Thornborrow notes, the implied British conception of security as "concrete, fixed, and immobile" contrasts deeply with the French conception of security as "a system as a series of processes."

Our ultimate goal is to use metaphor to further our knowledge of how different cultures understand complex topics. Our immediate goal in this paper is to create an automated system to find instances of metaphor in English and Spanish text.

Most existing work on metaphor identification (Fass, 1991; Martin, 1994; Peters and Peters, 2000; Mason, 2004; Birke and Sarkar, 2006; Gegigan et al., 2006; Krishnakumaran and Zhu, 2007; Shutova et al., 2010; Shutova et al., 2012)[1] has relied on some or all of handwritten rules, syntactic parsing, and semantic databases like WordNet (Fellbaum, 1998) and FrameNet (Baker et al., 1998). This limits the approaches to languages with rich linguistic resources. As our ultimate goal is broad, cross-linguistic application of our system, we cannot rely on resources which would be unavailable in resource-poor languages. Instead, we apply LDA topic modeling (Blei et al., 2003b) which requires only an adequate amount of raw text in the target language. This work is similar to Bethard et al. (2009), in which an SVM model is trained with LDA-based features to recognize metaphorical text. There the work is framed as a classification task, and supervised methods are used to label metaphorical and literal text. Here, the task is one of recognition, and we use heuristic-based, unsu-

[1] See Shutova (2010) for a survey of existing approaches

pervised methods to identify the presence of metaphor in unlabeled text. We hope to eliminate the need for labeled data which, as discussed in Bethard et al. (2009) and elsewhere, is very difficult to produce for metaphor recognition.

2 Terminology

We will refer to a particular instance of metaphorical language in text as a **linguistic metaphor**. Each such metaphor talks about a **target concept** in terms of a **source concept**. For example, in "Dems, like rats, will attack when cornered" the source concept is *animals* and the target concept is *politicians*[2], or at a higher level, *governance*. The abstract mapping between a source concept and a target concept will be referred to as a **conceptual metaphor** which is **grounded** by a collection of linguistic metaphors.

In this work, we restrict our attention to a single target concept, *governance*. Our definition of *governance* is broad, including views of the governed and those who govern, institutions of government, laws, and political discourse. We used a large collection (see **Table 1**) of potential source concepts. Beginning with the source concepts of **primary metaphors**, which are hypothesized to be universal (Grady, 1998), we expanded our set to include source concepts commonly found in the scientific literature about metaphor, as well as those found by human annotators manually collecting instances of governance-related metaphors.

Animals	Fishing	Plants
Baseball	Flight	Race
Body	Football	Religion
Botany	Gambling	Sick
Boundary	Grasp	Size
Chess	Health	Sound
Color	Height	Sports
Combustion	Light	Taste
Cooking	Liquid	Temperature
Courtship	Machine	Texture
Cut	Maritime	Theater
Directional force	Money	Time of day
Dogs	Motion	Toxicity
Drug use	Mythology	Vehicle
Electricity	Natural disasters	War
Energy source	Nuclear	Weaponry
Entry	Odor	Weather
Family	Pathways	Weight
Farming	Physical structure	Wild west
Fight	Planning	

Table 1: English Source Concepts

3 High-level system overview

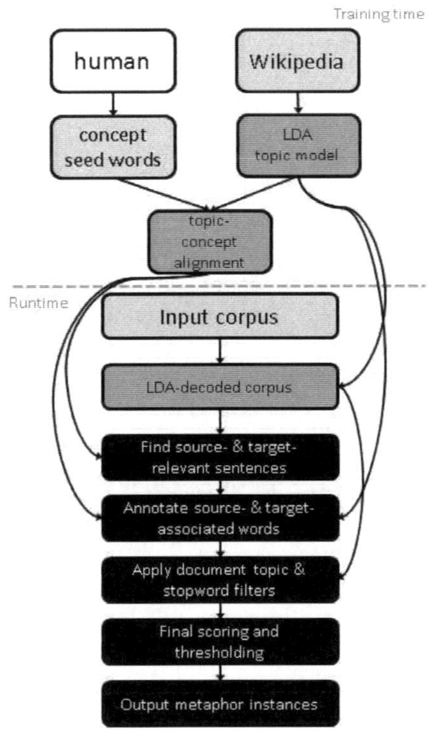

Figure 1: System Overview

Our main hypothesis is that metaphors are likely to be found in sentences that exhibit evidence of both a source and a target concept. The core idea of our system is to use LDA topics as proxies for semantic concepts which may serve as the source or target for a metaphor. For a given language, we build an LDA model from Wikipedia and then align its topics to potential source and target concepts, which are defined by small human-created lists of seed words.

At runtime, the system first does LDA inference on our input corpus to get topic probabilities for each document and sentence. The system then selects those sentences linked by LDA to both a source-aligned topic and a target-aligned topic.[3] For example, a sentence containing "*...virtud so-*

[2] "Dems"' refers to the Democratic Party, an American political party

[3] This is a distant, automatic relative of the 'directed-search' technique of Martin (1994).

cial para construir la democracia...'[4] will be selected because LDA strongly associates it with both the topic [*elecciones*, *ministro*, *sucesor*, ...][5], aligned to the target concept *governance*, and the topic [*edificio, arquitectura, torre,...*] [6], aligned to the source concept *physical structure.*

Next, the system identifies the words in each selected sentence that are strongly associated with each concept. In the sentence above, it marks *virtud* and *democracia* as target-associated and *construir* as source-associated.

Next it applies two filters. First, we exclude any sentence with too few words that are not LDA stopwords, because the model's predictions may be very inaccurate in these cases. Second, if the topic associated with the source model for a sentence is also a top-ranked topic for the document as a whole, the sentence is excluded. The reason for this is that if the source concept is present throughout the document, it is probably being used literally (see **Figure 2**).

Finally, it uses previously-computed information to determine a final score. All linguistic metaphors scoring above a certain threshold are returned. By varying this threshold, the user can vary the precision-recall tradeoff as needed. A diagram of the system can be found in **Figure 1**.

Our county has many roads in bad shape. Thousands of our bridges are structurally deficient. Congress needs to pass a new highway bill.

Figure 2: Even though the last sentence is relevant to the source concept *pathways* and the target concept *governance*, it will be correctly rejected because *pathways*-aligned topics are present throughout the document.

4 Implementation Details: Training

Our runtime system requires as input an LDA model, a list of seed words for each concept, and an alignment between concepts and LDA topics.

4.1 LDA Topic Model

The topics defined by LDA topic modeling serve as stand-ins for the more abstractly-defined source and target concepts underlying the metaphors. The input to training our LDA model is the full text of Wikipedia articles in the target language. Wikipedia is available in numerous languages and serves as a corpus of general knowledge, providing us with topics corresponding to a broad range of concepts. Our LDA model is trained using MALLET (McCallum, 2002) for 1000 iterations with 100 topics, optimizing hyperparameters every 10 iterations after a 100 iteration burn-in period. The 500 most common tokens in the training corpus were used as stopwords. The result of LDA is 100 topics, where each topic is a probability distribution over the training corpus vocabulary. Representative words for example English topics are shown in **Figure 3**.

theater stage musical miss actreess
theory philosophy pp study scientific knowledge
nfl bowl yards coach players card yard
governor republican senate election congress

Figure 3: Sample LDA topics with representative terms

4.2 Concept Seed Word Lists

For each concept c, we have a label and a small set of *seed words* representing that concept, referred to as $K(c)$. These lists were created by hand in English and then translated into Spanish by native speakers. The translation was not intended to be exact; we instructed the annotators to create the lists in a way that was appropriate for their language and culture. For instance, the *football* topic for English describes American football, but in Spanish, the same topic describes soccer.

4.3 Concept-Topic Alignment

The final input to our system is an alignment between concepts and topics, with every topic being mapped to at most one concept. In addition to the seed lists and LDA model, this alignment process takes a score threshold z_{align} and a maximum number of alignments per source and target concept N_S and N_T.

The alignment algorithm is as follows. We align each topic t to the concept c with the maximum score $\lambda(c,t)$, which measures the concept terms' summed probability in the LDA topic: $\lambda(c,t) = \sum_{w \in K(c)} p(w|t)$. We remove all alignments where $\lambda(c,t) < z_{align}$. Finally, for each concept, only the N highest scoring alignments are kept, where N may be different for source and

[4] social virtue to build democracy
[5] elections, minister, successor
[6] building, architecture, tower

target. We refer to the aligned topics for a concept c as $\Lambda(c)$.

Label	Seed List Words	Aligned Topics
Vehicle	***vehicle, wheels, gas, bus***	***0.035: engine, car, model***
		0.29: railway, trains, train
		0.022: energy, gas, linear
Animals	animal, beast, cattle	0.066: animals, animal, species
Courtship	courtship, romance, court	None
Governance	aristocrat, bipartisan, citizen, duke	0.25: Election, elected, parliament
		0.22: Governor, republican, Senate
		0.14: sir, lord, henry
		0.13: kingdom, emperor, empire
		0.12: rights, legal, laws

Table 2: Sample concepts, manually-created seed lists, and aligned topics

A last condition on the topic-concept alignment is the assignment of topics to *trump concepts*. Our only trump concept in this study is *war*. If an LDA topic is aligned with both the *war* concept and the *governance* concept, it is removed from alignment with the *governance* concept. We do this because *war* is so tightly associated with governments that the alignment algorithm invariably aligns it to the *governance* topic. However, *war* is also a very important source concept for *governance* metaphors; our choice is to suffer on recall by missing some governance-relevant sentences, but increase recall on metaphors for which the source concept is *war*. Sample topic-concept alignments are shown in**Table 2**. By inspecting the resulting alignments by hand, we chose the following parameter values for both languages: z_{align}=0.01, N_S=3, N_T=5.

The process of defining concepts is simple and fast and the alignment method is inexpensive. Therefore, while we have not captured all possible source concepts in our initial list, expanding this list is not difficult. We can define new source concepts iteratively as we analyze metaphors that our extraction system misses, and we can add target concepts as our interests broaden.

5 Implementation Details: Runtime

The system receives as input a corpus of documents, their LDA decodings, the LDA decodings of each sentence treated as a separate document, and the topic-concept alignments. Each four-tuple (L, S, T, x) is processed independently, where L is the language, S is the source concept, T is the target concept, and x is the sentence.

Determining Concept Relevance: Recall our basic intuition that a sentence relevant both to an LDA topic in $\Lambda(S)$ (termed **source-relevant**) and one in $\Lambda(T)$ (termed **target-relevant**) is potentially metaphorical. The system judges a sentence x to be C-relevant if the probability of C-aligned topics in that sentence is above a threshold: $\rho_C(x) = \sum_{t \in \Lambda(C)} p(t|x) \geq z_{rel,C}$, where $z_{rel,C}$ is an adjustable parameter tuned by hand. $z_{rel,S}$ is 0.06 in English and 0.05 in Spanish. $z_{rel,T}$ is 0.1 in both languages. On the source side, the system removes all topics in $\Lambda(T)$ from $p(t|x)$ and renormalizes before determining relevance in order to avoid penalizing sentences for having very strong evidence of relevance to governance in addition to providing evidence of relevance to a source concept. For reference below, let $\rho_{ST}(x) = \rho_S(x)\rho_T(x)$ (a measure of how strongly the sentence is associated with its topics) and let $R_C(x) = argmax_{t \in \Lambda(C)}\, p(t|x)$ (the most probable C-aligned topic in the sentence).

If x is not both source- and target-relevant, the system stops and the sentence is not selected.

Finding Concept-Associated Words: The system next creates sets A_C of the words in x associated with the concept C. Let $\sigma_C(w) = \sum_{t \in C} p(t|x)$. Then let $A'_C = \{w \in x \,|\sigma_C(w) \geq z_{word}\}$, where z_{word} is a hand tuned parameter set to 0.1 for both languages. That is, any word whose probability in the topic is higher than a theshold is included as a concept-associated word in that sentence. Let $A_S = A'_S - A'_T$ and vice-versa. Note that words which could potentially be associated with either concept are associated with neither. For reference below, let $\omega_C(w) = max_{w \in x}\, \sigma_C(w)$ (the most strongly concept-associated words in the sentence) and $\omega_{ST}(x) = \omega_S(x)\omega_T(x)$ (the combined strength of those associations).

If x lacks words strongly associated with the source and target concepts (that is, A_S or A_T is empty), the system stops and the sentence is not selected.

Filters: The system applies two filters. First, x must have at least four words which are not LDA stopwords; otherwise, the LDA predictions which drive the system's concept-relevance judgements tend to be unreliable. Second, the most likely source topic $R_S(x)$ must not be one of the top 10 topics for the document as a whole, for reasons described above. If either of these requirements fail, the system stops and the sentence is not selected.

Final Scoring: Finally, the system determines if

$$\ln\left(\lambda_S(R_S(x))\lambda_T(R_T(x))\rho_{ST}(x)\omega_{ST}(x)\right) > z_{final}$$

where z_{final} is a hand-tuned threshold set to -10.0 for English and -13.0 for Spanish. This takes into account the strength of association between topics and the sentence, between the annotated words and the topics, and between the topics and their aligned concepts. Any sentence passing this threshold is selected as a linguistic metaphor.

6 Example Output

We provide examples of both true and false positives extracted by our system. The annotations of source and target-associated words in each sentence are those defined as A_S and A_T above. The source concept *animals* is used for all examples.

1. **Moderates**$_T$ we all hear are an **endangered**$_S$ **species**$_S$, Sen. Richard
2. **Dems**$_T$ like **rats**$_S$ sometimes attack when cornered
3. **Obama**$_T$'s world historical political ambitions **crossbred**$_S$ with his
4. At least **Democratic**$_T$ **representatives**$_T$ are **snakehead**$_S$ fish
5. Another **whopper**$_S$ from Cleveland, **GOP**$_T$ lawyer backs him up
6. Previous post: Illinois **GOP**$_T$ **lawmaker**$_T$ arrested in **animal**$_S$ feed bag related incident
7. Next post: National Enquirer catfighting **Michelle Obama**$_T$ has **claws**$_S$ out for that nice Ann Romney
8. Sen. Lisa **Murkowski**$_T$ R AK independent from Alaska - thank you silly Repubs, **tea**$_S$ party her out ha

Examples 1 through 4 are correct metaphors extracted by our system. In each, some words related to the target concept *governance* are described using terms related to the source concept *animals*. Example 1 best represents the desired output of our system, such that it contains a governance- and animals-relevant metaphor and the terms associated with the metaphor are properly annotated. Some issues do arise in these true positive examples. Example 2, while often termed a simile, is counted as a metaphor for our purposes. In example 3, the source term is correctly annotated, but the target terms should be *political ambitions* rather than *Obama*. It is unclear why the term *snakehead* but not the term *fish* in example 4 is associated with the source concept.

Examples 5 through 8 represent system errors. In example 5, the fact that the word *whopper* occurs frequently to describe a large animal (especially a fish) causes the sentence to be mistakenly identified as relevant to the source concept *animal*. The source term *animal* in example 6 is clearly relevant to the source concept, but it is being used literally. The document-level source concept filtering does not entirely eliminate this error class. While example 7 contains a metaphor and has some relationship to American politics, it would be counted as an error in our evaluations because the metaphor itself is not related to *governance*. In example 8, we have two errors. First, *tea* is strongly present in the topic aligned to the *animal* concept, causing the sentence to be incorrectly marked as source-relevant. Second, because our topic model operates at the level of individual words, it was unable to recognize that *tea* here is part of the fixed, *governance*-related phrase *tea party*.[7]

7 Evaluation

7.1 Collecting Evaluation Data

We collected a domain-specific corpus in each language. We curated a set of news websites and governance-relevant blogs in English and Spanish and then collected data from these websites over the course of several months. For each language, we ran our system over this corpus (all steps in

[7] an American political movement

Section 5), produced a set of linguistic metaphors for each topic-aligned source concept (the target concept was always *governance*), and ranked them by the final score (Section 4.4). Below, we will refer to the set of all linguistic metaphors sharing the same source and target concept as a conceptual metaphor.

7.2 Simple Evaluation

For this evaluation, we selected the top five examples for each conceptual metaphor. If the same sentence was selected by multiple conceptual metaphors, it was kept for only the highest scoring one. We then added enough of the highest-ranked unselected metaphors to create a full set of 300. We then added random sentences from the corpus that were *not* selected as metaphorical by the system to bring the total to 600. Our Spanish annotators were unavailable at the time this evaluation took place, so we are only able to report results for English in this case.

For each of these instances, two annotators were asked the question, "Is there a metaphor about governance in this example?" These annotators had previous experience in identifying metaphors for this study, both by searching manually in online texts and evaluating previous versions of our system. Over time we have given them feedback on what does and does not constitute a metaphor. In this case, the annotators were given neither the system's concept-word association annotations nor the source concept associated with the instance. In one way, the evaluation was generous, because any metaphor in the extracted sentence would benefit precision even if it was not the metaphor found by our system. On the other hand, the same is true for the random sentences; while the system will only extract metaphors with source concepts in our list, the annotators had no such restriction. This causes the recall score to suffer. The annotation task was difficult, with a κ-score of 0.48. The resulting scores are given in **Table 3**. The examples given in Section 5 illustrate the error classes found among the false positives identified by the human annotators. There are many cases where the source-concept associated terms are used literally rather than metaphorically, and many cases where the system-found metaphor is not about governance. Some text processing issues, such as a bug in our sentence breaking script, as well as the noisy nature of blog and blog comment input, caused some of the examples to be difficult to interpret or evaluate.

Annotator	Precision	'Recall'	F	Kappa
1	65	67	66	0.48
2	43	60	50	
Mean	54	64	59	

Table 3: Simple English Evaluation

7.3 Stricter Evaluation

Common Experimental Setup

We did a second evaluation of both English and Spanish using a different paradigm. For each language, we selected the 250 highest-ranked linguistic metaphor instances in the corpus. Subjects on Amazon Mechanical Turk were shown instances with the system-predicted concept-associated words highlighted and asked if the highlighted words were being used metaphorically (options were *yes* and *no*). Each subject was randomly asked about roughly a quarter of the data.

We paid the subjects $10 per hour. We added catch trial sentences which asked the subject to simply answer *yes* or *no* as a way of excluding those not actually reading the sentences. Subjects answering these questions incorrectly were excluded (17 in English, 25 in Spanish).

We defined the **metaphoricity** of an instance to be the fraction of subjects who answered *yes* for that instance. We define the metaphoricity of a conceptual metaphor as the average metaphoricity of its groundings among the instances in this evaluation set.

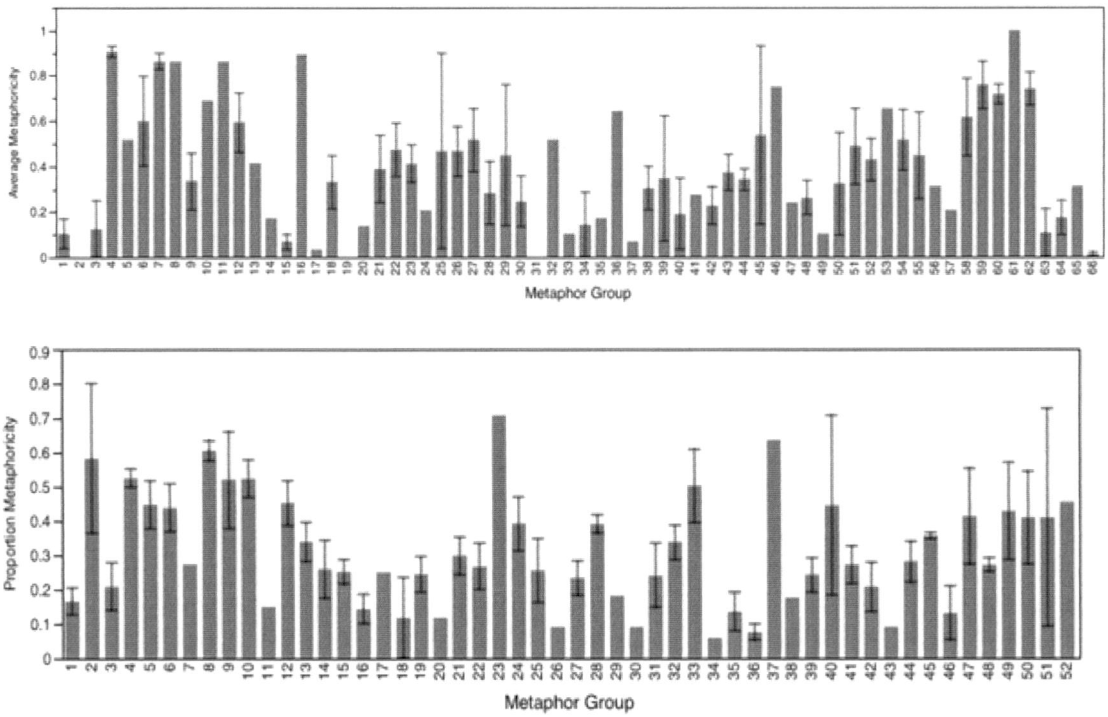

Figure 4: Metaphoricity of Conceptual Metaphors for English (top) and Spanish (bottom)

English Results

We restricted our subjects to those claiming to be native English speakers who had IP addresses within the U.S. and had 115 participants. The examples were grouped into 66 conceptual metaphors. The mean metaphoricity of instances was 0.41 (standard deviation=0.33). The mean metaphoricity of the conceptual metaphors (**Figure 4**), was 0.39 (SD=0.26). Although there was wide variance in metaphoricity across conceptual metaphors, it appears likely that most of the conceptual metaphors discovered by the system are correct: 65% of the conceptual metaphors had metaphoricity greater than 0.25, and 73% greater than 0.2. Given that many metaphors are conventional and difficult to detect in natural language (Lakoff and Johnson, 1980), it is possible that even in cases in which only a minority of subjects detected a metaphor, a metaphor nonetheless exists

Spanish Results

We restricted our subjects to those claiming to be native speakers of Mexican Spanish with IP addresses in the US (57) or Mexico (29). The instances were grouped into 52 conceptual metaphors. The mean metaphoricity of instances was 0.33 (SD=0.23) and for conceptual metaphors (**Figure 4**), 0.31 (SD=0.16). 60% of conceptual metaphors had metaphoricity greater than 0.25, and 73% greater than 0.2. That performance was only slightly lower than English is a positive indication of our method's cross-linguistic potential.

8 Discussion and Future Work

We observed a number of problems with our approach which provide avenues for future research.

8.1 Topics as Proxies of Primary Metaphor Concepts

Many of the metaphors missed by our system were instances of primary metaphor, especially those involving movement and spatial position. Our LDA approach is poorly suited to these because the source concepts are not well-characterized by word co-occurrence: words describing movement and spatial position do not have a strong tendency to co-occur with other such words, at least in Wikipedia. Augmenting our system with a separate approach to primary metaphor would boost its performance significantly.

8.2 Topics as Proxies of Non-Primary Metaphor Concepts

We found that most of our potential source concepts did not correspond to any LDA topic. However, many of these, such as *wild west*, have fairly strong word co-occurrence patterns, so they plausibly could be found by a different topic modeling algorithm. There are two promising approaches here which could potentially be combined. The first is to use a hierarchical LDA algorithm (Blei et al, 2003b) to allow concepts to align to topics with varying degrees of granularity, from the very general (e.g. *war*) to the very specific (e.g. *wild west*). The second is to use constrained LDA approaches (Andrzejewski and Zhu, 2009; Hu et al., 2010) to attempt to force at least one topic to correspond to each of our seed concept lists.

A different approach would leave behind seed lists entirely. In our current approach, only about one third of the topics modeled by LDA are successfully aligned with a source concept from our hand-made list. However, some non-aligned LDA topics have properties similar to those that were chosen to represent source concepts. For instance, the topic whose highest ranked terms are [*institute, professor, engineering, degree*] is comprised of a set of semantically coherent and concrete terms, and could be assigned a reasonably accurate label such as *higher education*. If we were to choose LDA topics based on the terms' coherence and concreteness (and perhaps other relevant, measurable properties), then assign a label using a method such as that in Mei et al. (2007), we would be able to leverage more of the concepts in the LDA model. This would increase the recall of our system, and also reduce some of the confusion associated with incorrect labeling of concepts in linguistic and conceptual metaphors. Applying Labeled LDA, as in Ramage et al. (2009), would be a similar approach.

8.3 Confusion of Literal and Metaphorical Usage of Source Concepts

Another major problem was the confusion between literal and metaphorical usage of source terms. This is partly addressed by our document topics filter, but more sophisticated use of document context for this purpose would be helpful. A similar filter based on contexts across the test corpus might be useful.

8.4 Fixed Expressions

Some of our errors were due to frequent fixed phrases which included a word strongly associated with a source topic, like *Tea Party*. Minimum description length (MDL) phrase-finding or similar techniques could be used to filter these out. Initial experiments performed after the evaluations discussed above show promise in this regard. Using the MDL algorithm (Rissanen, 1978), we developed a list of likely multi-word expressions in the Wikipedia corpus. We then concatenated these phrases in the Wikipedia corpus before LDA modeling and in the test corpus before metaphor prediction. Though we did not have time to formally evaluate the results, a subjective analysis showed fewer of these fixed phrases appearing as indicators of metaphor (as words in A_s or A_T).

8.5 Difficulty of Annotation

A different method of presentation of metaphors to the subjects, for instance with annotations marking where in the sentence we believed metaphor to exist or with a suggestion of the source concept, may have improved agreement and perhaps the system's evaluation score.

8.6 Summary

We have presented a technique for linguistic and conceptual metaphor discovery that is cross-linguistically applicable and requires minimal linguistic resources. Our approach of looking for overlapping semantic concepts allows us to find metaphors of any syntactic structure. The framework of our metaphor discovery technique is flexible in its ability to incorporate a wide variety of source and target concepts. The only linguistic resources the system requires are a corpus of general-knowledge text adequate for topic modeling and a small set of seed word lists. We could improve our system by applying new research in automatic topic modeling, by creating new filters and scoring mechanisms to discriminate between literal and figurative word usages, and by creating training data to allow us to automatically set certain system parameters.

Acknowledgements

Supported by the Intelligence Advanced Research Projects Activity (IARPA) via Department of Defense US Army Research Laboratory contract number **W911NF-12-C0-0023**. The U.S. Government is authorized to reproduce and distribute reprints for Governmental purposes notwithstanding any copyright annotation thereon. Disclaimer: The views and conclusions contained herein are those of the authors and should not be interpreted as necessarily representing the official policies or endorsements, either expressed or implied, of IARPA, DoD/ARL, or the U.S. Government."

References

David Andrzejewski and Xiaojin Zhu. 2009. Latent Dirichlet Allocation with Topic-in-Set Knowledge. In *Proceedings of NAACL Workshop on Semi-Supervised Learning for NLP.*

Collin Baker, Charles Fillmore, and John Lowe. 1998. The Berkeley FrameNet project. In *Proceedings of COLING-ACL.*

Stephen Bethard, Vicky Tzuyin Lai and James H. Martin. 2009. Topic Model Analysis of Metaphor Frequency for Psycholinguistic Stimuli. . In *Proc. Of NAACL-HLT Workshop on Computational Approaches to Linguistic Creativity.*

Julia Birke and Anoop Sarkar. 2006. A Clustering Approach for the Nearly Unsupervised Recognition of Nonliteral Language. In *Proceedings of EACL.*

David Blei, Thomas Griffiths, Michael Jordan, and Joshua Tenenbaum. 2003a. Hierarchical topic models and the nested Chinese restaurant process. In *Proceedings of NIPS.*

David Blei, Andrew Ng, and Michael Jordan. 2003b. Latent Dirichlet Allocation. *Journal of Machine Learning Research*, 2003(3):993–1022.

Dan Fass. 1991. met*: A Method for Discriminating Metonymy and Metaphor by Computer. *Computational Linguistics*, 17(1):49–90.

Christine Fellbaum. 1998. WordNet: An Electronic Lexical Database. MIT Press, Cambridge, MA.

Matt Gegigan, John Bryant, Srini Narayanan, and Branimir Ciric. 2006. Catching Metaphors. In *Proceedings of the 3rd Workshop on Scalable Natural Language Understanding.*

Joseph E. Grady. 1998. Foundations of meaning: Primary metaphors and primary scenes. UMI.

Yuenin Hu, Jordan Boyd-Graber, and Brianna Satinoff. 2010. Interactive Topic Modeling. In *Proceedings of ACL.*

Saisuresh Krishnakumaran and Xiaojin Zhu. 2007. Hunting Elusive Metaphors Using Lexical Resources. In *Proceedings of the Workshop on Computational Approaches to Figurative Language.*

George Lakoff and Mark Johnson. 1980. Metaphors We Live By. University of Chicago.

James H. Martin. 1994. MetaBank: A knowledge-base of metaphoric language convention. *Computational Intelligence*, 10(2):134–149.

Zachary Mason. 2004. CorMet: A Computational, Corpus-Based Conventional Metaphor Extraction System. *Computational Linguistics*, 30(1):23–44.

Andrew Kachites McCallum. 2002. MALLET: A Machine Learning for Language Toolkit. http://mallet.cs.umass.edu.

Qiaozhu Mei, Xuehua Shen, and Chengxiang Zhai. Automatic Labeling of Multinomial Topic Models. In *Proceedings of KDD '07.* 2007.

Wim Peters and Ivonne Peters. 2000. Lexicalised Systematic Polysemy in WordNet. In *Proceedings of LREC.*

Daniel Ramage, David Hall, Ramesh Nallapati and Christopher D. Manning. 2009. Labeled LDA: A supervised topic model for credit attribution in multi-labeled corpora. In *Proceedings of EMNLP.*

Jorma Rissanen. Modeling by shortest data description. *Automatica* 14:465-471.

Ekaterina Shutova, Lin Sun, and Anna Korhonen. 2010. Metaphor Identification Using Noun and Verb Clustering. In *Proceedings of COLING.*

Ekaterina Shutova, Simone Teufel, and Anna Korhonen. 2012. Statistical Metaphor Processing. *Computational Linguistics.* Uncorrected proof.

Ekaterina Shutova. 2010. Models of metaphor in NLP. In *Proceedings of ACL.*

Joanna Thornborrow. 1993. Metaphors of security: a comparison of representation in defence discourse in post-cold-war France and Britain. *Discource & Society*, 4(1):99–119

Robust Extraction of Metaphors from Novel Data

Tomek Strzalkowski[1], George Aaron Broadwell[1], Sarah Taylor[2], Laurie Feldman[1], Boris Yamrom[1], Samira Shaikh[1], Ting Liu[1], Kit Cho[1], Umit Boz[1], Ignacio Cases[1] and Kyle Elliott[3]

[1]State University of New York
University at Albany
Albany NY USA 12222
tomek@albany.edu

[2]Sarah M. Taylor Consulting LLC
121 South Oak St.
Falls Church VA USA 22046
talymail59@gmail.com

[3]Plessas Experts
Network Inc.
Herndon VA 20171
kelliot@plessas.net

Abstract

This article describes our novel approach to the automated detection and analysis of metaphors in text. We employ robust, quantitative language processing to implement a system prototype combined with sound social science methods for validation. We show results in 4 different languages and discuss how our methods are a significant step forward from previously established techniques of metaphor identification. We use Topical Structure and Tracking, an Imageability score, and innovative methods to build an effective metaphor identification system that is fully automated and performs well over baseline.

1 Introduction

The goal of this research is to automatically identify metaphors in textual data. We have developed a prototype system that can identify metaphors in naturally occurring text and analyze their semantics, including the associated affect and force. Metaphors are mapping systems that allow the semantics of a familiar Source domain to be applied to a Target domain so that new frameworks of reasoning can emerge in the Target domain. Metaphors are pervasive in discourse, used to convey meanings indirectly. Thus, they provide critical insights into the preconceptions, assumptions and motivations underlying discourse, especially valuable when studied across cultures. When metaphors are thoroughly understood within the context of a culture, we gain substantial knowledge about cultural values. These insights can help better shape cross-cultural understanding and facilitate discussions and negotiations among different communities.

A longstanding challenge, however, is the large-scale, automated identification of metaphor in volumes of data, and especially the interpretation of their complex, underlying semantics.

We propose a data-driven computational approach that can be summarized as follows: Given textual input, we first identify any sentence that contains references to Target concepts in a given Target Domain (Target concepts are elements that belong to a particular domain; for instance "government bureaucracy" is a Target concept in the "Governance" domain). We then extract a passage of length 2N+1, where N is the number of sentences preceding (or succeeding) the sentence with Target Concept. We employ dependency parsing to determine the syntactic structure of each input sentence. Topical structure and imageability analysis are then combined with dependency parsing output to locate the candidate metaphorical expressions within a sentence. For this step, we identify nouns and verbs in the passage (of length 2N+1) and link their occurrences – including repetitions, pronominal references, synonyms and hyponyms. This linking uncovers the topical structure that holds the narrative together. We then locate content words that are outside the topical structure and compute their imageability scores. Any nouns or adjectives outside the main topical structure that also have high imageability scores and are dependency-linked in the parse structure to the Target Concept are identified as candidate *source relations*, i.e., expressions borrowed from a Source domain to describe the Target concept. In addition, any verbs that have a direct dependency on the Target Concept are considered as candidate relations. These candidate relations are then used to compute and rank proto-sources. We search for their arguments in a balanced corpus, assumed to represent standard use of the language, and cluster the results. Proto-source clusters and their ranks are exploited to determine whether the candidate relations are metaphorical or literal. Finally, we compute the affect and force associated with the metaphor.

Our approach is shown to work in four languages – American English, Mexican Spanish, Russian Russian and Iranian Farsi. We detail in this paper the application of our approach to detection of metaphors using specific examples from the "Governance" domain. However, our approach can be expanded to work on extracting metaphors in any domain, even unspecified ones. We shall briefly explain this in Section 5; we defer the details of the expanded version of the algorithm to a separate larger publication. In addition, we shall primarily present examples in English to illustrate details of our algorithms. However, modules for all four languages have the same implementation in our system.

The rest of the paper is organized as follows: in Section 2, we discuss related research in this field. Section 3 presents our approach in detail; Section 4 describes our evaluation and results. In Section 5 we discuss our conclusions and future directions.

2 Related Work

Most current research on metaphor falls into three groups: (1) theoretical linguistic approaches (as defined by Lakoff & Johnson, 1980; and their followers) that generally look at metaphors as abstract language constructs with complex semantic properties; (2) quantitative linguistic approaches (e.g., Charteris-Black, 2002; O'Halloran, 2007) that attempt to correlate metaphor semantics with their usage in naturally occurring text but generally lack robust tools to do so; and (3) social science approaches, particularly in psychology and anthropology that seek to explain how people deploy and understand metaphors in interaction, but which lack the necessary computational tools to work with anything other than relatively isolated examples.

Metaphor study in yet other disciplines has included cognitive psychologists (e.g., Allbritton, McKoon & Gerrig, 1995) who have focused on the way metaphors may signify structures in human memory and human language processing. Cultural anthropologists, such as Malkki in her work on refugees (1992), see metaphor as a tool to help outsiders interpret the feelings and mindsets of the groups they study, an approach also reflective of available metaphor case studies, often with a Political Science underpinning (Musolff, 2008; Lakoff, 2001).

In computational investigations of metaphor, knowledge-based approaches include MetaBank (Martin, 1994), a large knowledge base of metaphors empirically collected. Krishnakumaran and Zhu (2007) use WordNet (Felbaum, 1998) knowledge to differentiate between metaphors and literal usage. Such approaches entail the existence of lexical resources that may not always be present or satisfactorily robust in different languages. Gedigan et al (2006) identify a system that can recognize metaphor. However their approach is only shown to work in a narrow domain (Wall Street Journal, for example).

Computational approaches to metaphor (largely AI research) to date have yielded only limited scale, often hand designed systems (Wilks, 1975; Fass, 1991; Martin, 1994; Carbonell, 1980; Feldman & Narayan, 2004; Shutova & Teufel, 2010; inter alia, also Shutova, 2010b for an overview). Baumer et al (2010) used semantic role labels and typed dependency parsing in an attempt towards computational metaphor identification. However they self-report their work to be an initial exploration and hence, inconclusive. Shutova et al (2010a) employ an unsupervised method of metaphor identification using nouns and verb clustering to automatically impute metaphoricity in a large corpus using an annotated training corpus of metaphors as seeds. Their method relies on annotated training data, which is difficult to produce in large quantities and may not be easily generated in different languages.

By contrast, we propose an approach that is fully automated and can be validated using empirical social science methods. Details of our algorithm follow next.

3 Our Approach

In this section, we walk through the steps of metaphor identification in detail. Our overall algorithm consists of five main steps from obtaining textual input to classification of input as metaphorical or literal.

3.1 Passage Identification

The input to our prototype system is a piece of text. This text may be taken from any genre – news articles, blogs, magazines, official announcements, broadcast transcripts etc.

Given the text, we first identify sentences that contain Target concepts in the domain we are interested in. Target concepts are certain keywords that occur within the given domain and represent concepts that may be targets of metaphor. For instance, in the "Governance" domain, concepts such as "federal bureaucracy" and "state mandates" serve as Target concepts. We keep a list of Target concepts to search through when analyzing given input. This list can be automatically created by mining Target Concepts from resource such as Wikipedia, given the Target domain, or manually constructed. Space limits the discussion of how such lists may be automatically created; a separate larger publication addresses our approach to this task in greater detail.

In Figure 1, we show a piece of text drawn from a 2008 news article. The sentence in italics contains one of our Target concepts: "federal bureaucracy". We extract the sentence containing Target concepts that match any of those in our list, including N sentences before and N sentences after the sentence if they exist, to yield a passage of at most 2N+1 sentences. For the example shown in Figure 1, the Target concept is "federal bureaucracy". In current system prototype, N=2. Hence, we extract two sentences prior to the sentence containing "federal bureaucracy" (in Figure 1 example, these are omitted for ease of presentation) and two sentences following the given sentence.

Once this passage is extracted, we need to determine whether a metaphor is present in the middle sentence. To accomplish that, we follow the steps as described in the next section.

These qualities[1] have helped him[4] ***navigate the labyrinthine*** *federal bureaucracy in his demanding $191,300-a-year job as the top federal official[3] responsible for bolstering airline, border[2], port and rail security against a second catastrophic terrorist attack.*
But those same personal qualities[1] also explain why the 55-year-old Cabinet officer[3] has alienated so many Texans along the U.S.-Mexico border[2] with his[4] relentless implementation of the Bush administration's hard-nosed approach to immigration enforcement - led by his unyielding push to construct 670 miles of border[2] fencing by the end of the year.
Some Texas officials are so exasperated that they say they'll just await the arrival of the next president before revisiting border enforcement with the federal government.

Figure 1. Excerpt from news article. Passage containing target concept highlighted in italics. The callouts [1], [2] etc., indicate topic chains (see next section).

3.2 Topical Structure and Imageability Analysis

Our hypothesis is that metaphorically used terms are typically found outside the topical structure of the text. This is an entirely novel method of effectively selecting candidate relations. It draws on Broadwell et al. (2012), who proposed a method to establish the topic chains in discourse as a means of modeling associated socio-linguistic phenomena such as topic control and discourse cohesiveness. We adapted this method to identify and exclude any words that serve to structure the core discussion, since the metaphorical words, except in the cases of extended and highly elaborated metaphors, are not the main subject, and thus unlikely to be repeated or referenced in the context surrounding the sentence.

We link the occurrences of each noun and verb in the passage (5 sentence length). Repetitions via synonyms, hyponyms, lexical variants and pronoun references are linked together. These words, as elements of the several topic chains in a text, are then excluded from further consideration. WordNet (Felbaum, 1998) is used to look up synonyms and hyponyms of the remaining content words. We illustrate this in Figure 1. We show the two sentences that form the latter context in the example passage. We show four of the topic chains discovered in this passage. These have been labeled via superscripts in Figure 1. [1] and [2] are the repetitions of word "qualities" and "border". The [3] identifies repetition via lexical variants "officer" and "official" and [4] identifies the pronoun co-references "him" and "his". We shall exclude these words from consideration when searching for candidate metaphorical relations in the middle sentence of the passage.

To further narrow the pool of candidate relations in this sentence, we compute the imageability scores of the remaining words. The hypothesis is metaphors use highly imageable words to convey their meaning. The use of imageability scores for the primary purpose of metaphor detection distinguishes our approach from other research on this problem. While Turney et al. (2011) explored the use of word concreteness (a concept related but not identical to imageability) in an attempt to disambiguate between abstract and concrete verb senses, their method was not specifically applied to detection of metaphors; rather it was used to classify verb senses for the purpose of resolving textual entailment. Broadwell et al. (2013) present a detailed description of our approach and how we use imageability scores to detect metaphors.

Our assertion is that any highly imageable word is more likely to be a metaphorical relation. We use the MRCPD (Coltheart 1981, Wilson 1988) expanded lexicon to look up the imageability scores of words not excluded via the topic chains. Although the MRCPD contains data for over 150,000 words, a major limitation of the database for our purposes is that the MRCPD has imageability ratings (i.e., how easily and quickly the word evokes a mental image) for only ~9,240 (6%) of the total words in its database. To fill this gap, we expanded the MRCPD database by adding imagery ratings for an further 59,989 words. This was done by taking the words for which the MRCPD database has an imageability rating and using that word as an index to synsets determined using WordNet (Miller, 1995). The expansion and validation of the expanded MRCPD imageability rating is presented in a separate, future publication.

Words that have an imageability rating lower than an experimentally determined threshold are further excluded from consideration. In the example shown in Figure 1, words that have sufficiently high imageability scores are "labyrinthine", "port", "rail" and "airline". We shall consider them as candidate relations, to be further investigated, as explained in the dependency parsing step described next.

3.3 Relation Extraction

Dependency parsing reveals the syntactic structure of the sentence with the Target concept. We use the Stanford parser (Klein and Manning, 2003) for English language data. We identify candidate metaphorical relations to be any verbs that have the Target concept in direct dependency path (other than auxiliary and modal verbs). We exclude verbs of attitude ("think", "say", "consider"), since these have been found to be more indicative of metonymy than of metaphor. This list of attitude verbs is automatically derived from WordNet.

From the example shown in Figure 1, one of the candidate relations extracted would be the verb "navigate".

In addition, we have a list of candidate relations from Step 3.2, which are the highly imageable nouns and adjectives that remain after topical structure analysis. Since "port", "rail" and "airline" do not have a direct dependency path to our Target concept of "federal bureaucracy", we drop these from further consideration. The highly imageable word remaining in this list is "labyrinthine".

Thus, two candidate relations are extracted from this passage – "navigate" and "labyrinthine". We shall now show how we use these to discover proto-sources for the potential metaphor.

3.4 Discovery of Proto-sources

Once candidate relations are identified, we examine whether the usage of these relations is metaphorical or literal. To determine this, we search for all uses of these relations in a balanced corpus and examine in which contexts the candidate relations occur. To demonstrate this via our example, we shall consider one of the candidate relations identified in Figure 1 – "navigate"; the search method is the same for all candidate relations identified. In the case of the verb "navigate" we search a balanced corpus for the collocated words, that is, those that occur within a 4-word window following the verb, with high mutual information (>3) and occurring together in the corpus with a frequency at least 3. This search returns a list of words, mostly nouns in this case, that are the objects of the verb "navigate", just as "federal bureaucracy" is the object in the given example. However, since the search occurs in a balanced corpus, given the parameters we search for, we discover words where the objects are literally navigated. Given these search parameters, the top results we get are generally literal uses of the word "navigate". We cluster the resulting literal uses as semantically related words using WordNet and corpus statistics. Each such cluster is an emerging prototype source domain, or a proto-source, for the potential metaphor.

In Figure 2, we show three of the clusters obtained when searching for the literal usage of the verb "navigate". We use elements of the clusters to give names or label the proto-source domains. WordNet hypernyms or synonyms are used in most cases. The clusters shown in Figure 2 represent three potential source domains for the given example, the labels "MAZE", "WAY" and "COURSE" are derived from WordNet.

1. Proto-source Name: **MAZE**
Proto-source Elements: [mazes, system, networks]
IMG Score: 0.74
2. Proto-source Name: **WAY**
Proto-source Elements: [way, tools]
IMG Score: 0.60
3. Proto-source Name: **COURSE**
Proto-source Elements: [course, streams]
IMG: 0.55

Figure 2. Three of several clusters obtained from balanced corpus search for objects of verb "navigate".

We rank the clusters according to the combined frequency of cluster elements in the balanced corpus. In a similar fashion, clusters are obtained for the candidate relation "labyrinthine"; however here we search for the nouns modified by the adjective "labyrinthine".

3.5 Estimation of Linguistic Metaphor

A ranked list of proto-sources from the previous step serves as evidence for the presence of a metaphor.

If any Target domain elements are found in the top two ranked clusters, we consider the phrase being investigated to be literal. This eliminates examples where one of the most frequently encountered sources is within the target domain.

If neither of the top two most frequent clusters contains any elements from the target domain, we then compute the average imageability scores for each cluster from the mean imageability score of the cluster elements. If no cluster has a sufficiently high imageability score (experimentally determined to be >.50 in the current prototype), we again consider the given input to be literal. This step reinforces the claim that metaphors use highly imageable language to convey their meaning. If a proto-source cluster is found to meet both criteria, we consider the given phrase to be metaphorical. For the example shown in Figure 1, our system finds "navigate the ...federal bureaucracy" to be metaphorical. One of the top Source domains identified for this metaphor is "MAZE". Hence the conceptual metaphor output for this example can be:

"FEDERAL BUREAUCRACY IS A MAZE".

Our system can thus classify input sentences as metaphorical or literal by the series of steps outlined above. In addition, we have modules that can determine a more complex conceptual metaphor, based upon evidence of one or more metaphorical passages as identified above. We do not discuss those modules in this article. Once a metaphor is identified, we compute associated Mappings, Affect and Force.

3.6 Mappings

In the current prototype system, we assign metaphors to one of three types of mappings. Propertive mappings – which state what the domain objects

Relation type	**Type 1 (property)** $T \rightarrow Rel$	**Type 2 (agentive)** $T \rightarrow Rel \rightarrow X$		**Type 3 (patientive)** $X \rightarrow Rel \rightarrow T$	
Relation/X		$X \geq neutral$	$X < neutral$	$X \geq neutral$	$X < neutral$
Rel > Positive	POSITIVE	POSITIVE	≤ UNSYMP	POSITIVE	≤ SYMPAT
Rel < Negative	NEGATIVE	≤ UNSYMP	≥ SYMPAT	≥ SYMPAT	≥ SYMPAT
Rel = Neutral	NEUTRAL	NEUTRAL	≤ NEUTRAL	NEUTRAL	≤ NEUTRAL

Table 1. Algorithm assigns affect of metaphor based upon mappings.

are and descriptive features; Agentive mappings – which describe what the domain elements do to other objects in the same or different domains; and Patientive mappings – which describe what is done to the objects in these domains. These are broad categories to which relations can, with some exceptions be assigned at the linguistic metaphor level by the parse tag of the relation. Relations that take Target concepts as objects are usually Patientive relations. Similarly, relations that are Agentive take Target concepts as subjects. Propertive relations are usually determined by adjectival relations.

Once mappings are assigned, we can use them to group linguistic metaphors. A set of linguistic metaphors on the same or semantically equivalent Target concepts can be grouped together if the relations are all agentive, patientive or propertive. The mapping assigned to set of examples in Figure 3 is Patientive.

One immediate consequence of the proposed approach is the simplicity with which we can represent domains, their elements, and the metaphoric mappings between domains. Regardless of what specific relations may operate within a domain (be it Source or Target), they can be classified into just 3 categories. We are further expanding this module to include semantically richer distinctions within the mappings. This includes the determination of the sub-dimensions of mappings i.e. assigning groups of relations to a semantic category.

3.7 Affect and Force

Affect of a metaphor may be positive, negative or neutral. Our affect estimation module computes an affect score taking into account the relation, Target concept and the subject or object of the relation based on the dependency between relation and Target concept. The algorithm is applied according to the categories shown in Table 1.

The expanded ANEW lexicon (Bradley and Lang, 2010) is used to look up affect scores of words. ANEW assigns scores from 0 (highly negative) to 9 (highly positive); 5 being neutral. We compute the affect of a metaphorical phrase within a sentence by summing the affect scores of the relation and its object or subject. If the relation is agentive, we then look at the object in source domain that the Target concept is acting upon. If the object (denoted in above table as X) has an affect score that is greater than neutral, and the relation itself has an affect score that is greater than neutral, then a POSITIVE affect is assigned to the metaphor. This is denoted by the cell at the intersection of the row labeled "Rel > Positive" and the 3rd column in Table 1. Similarly affect for the other mapping categories can be assigned.

1. His attorney described him as a family man who was lied to by a friend and who got **tangled in** federal bureaucracy he knew nothing about.
2. The chart, composed of 207 boxes illustrates the **maze of** federal bureaucracy that would have been created by then-President Bill Clinton's relation health reform plan in the early 1990s.
3. "Helping my constituents **navigate** the federal bureaucracy is one of the most important things I can do," said Owens.
4. A Virginia couple has donated $1 million to help start a center at Arkansas State University meant to help wounded veterans **navigate** the federal bureaucracy as they return to civilian life.

Figure 3. Four metaphors for the Target concept "federal bureaucracy".

We also seek to determine the impact of metaphor on the reader. This is explored using the concept of Force in our system. The force of a metaphor is estimated currently by the commonness of the expression in the given Target domain. We compute the frequency of the relation co-occurring with Target concept in a corpus of documents in the given Target domain. This frequency represents the commonness of expression, which is the inverse of Force. The more common a metaphorical expression is, the lesser its force.

For the example shown below in Figure 4, the affect is computed to be positive ("navigate" and "veterans" are both found to have positive affect scores, the relation is patientive). The force of this expression is low, since its commonness is 742 (commonness score > 100 is high commonness, determined experimentally).

A Virginia couple has donated $1 million to help start a center at Arkansas State University meant to help wounded *veterans* **navigate** the federal bureaucracy as they return to civilian life.

Figure 4. Example of metaphor with positive affect and low force.

The focus of this article is the automatic identification of metaphorical sentences in naturally occurring text. Affect and force modules are utilized to understand metaphors in context and contrast them across cultures, if feasible. We defer more detailed discussion of affect and force and their implications to a future, larger article.

4 Evaluation and Results

In order to determine the efficacy of our system in classifying metaphors as well as to validate various system modules such as affect and force, we performed a series of experiments to collect human validation of metaphors in a large set of examples.

4.1 Experimental Setup

We constructed validation tasks that aimed at performing evaluation of linguistic metaphor extraction accuracy. The first task – Task 1, consists of a series of examples, typically 50, split more or less equally between those proposed by the system to be metaphorical and those proposed to be literal. This task was designed to elicit subject and expert judgments on several aspects related to the presence or absence of linguistic metaphors in text. Subjects are presented with brief passages where a Target concept and a relation are highlighted. They are asked to rank their responses on a 7-point scale for the following questions:

Q1: To what degree does the above passage use metaphor to describe the highlighted concept?
Q2: To what degree does this passage convey an idea that is either positive or negative?
Q3: To what degree is it a common way to express this idea?

There are additional questions that ask subjects to judge the imageability and arousal of a given passage, which we do not discuss in this article. Q1 deals with assessing the metaphoricity of the example, Q2 deals with affect and Q3 deals with force.

Each instance of Task 1 consists of a set of instructions, training examples, and a series of passages to be judged. Instructions provide training examples whose ratings fall at each end the rating continuum. Following the task, participants take a grammar test to demonstrate native language proficiency in the target language. All task instances are then posted on Amazon's Mechanical Turk. The goal is to collect at least 30 valid judgments per task instance. We typically collect ~50 judgments from Mechanical Turkers, so that after filtering for invalid data which includes turkers selecting items at random, taking too little time to complete the task, grammar test failures, and other inconsistent data, we would still retain 30 valid judgments per passage. In addition to grammar test and time filter, we also inserted instance of known metaphors and known literal passages randomly within the Task. Any turker judgments that classify these known instance incorrectly more than 30% of the total known instance size are discarded.

The valid turker judgments are then converted to a binary judgment for the questions we presented. For example, for question Q1, the anchors to 7-point scale are 0 (none at all i.e. literal) to 7 (highly i.e metaphorical). We take [0, 2] as a literal judgment and [4, 6] as metaphorical and take a majority vote. If the majority vote is 3, we discard that passage from our test set, since it is undetermined whether the passage is literal or metaphorical.

We have collected human judgments on hundreds of metaphors in all four languages of interest. In Section 4.3, we explain our performance and compare our results to baseline where appropriate.

4.2 Test Reliability

The judgments collected from subjects are tested for reliability and validity. Reliability among the raters is computed by measuring intra-class correlation (ICC) (McGraw & Wong, 1996; Shrout & Fleiss, 1979). A coefficient value above 0.7 indicates strong reliability.

Table 3 shows the current reliability coefficients established for the selected Task 1 questions in all 4 languages. In general, our analyses have shown that with approximately 30 or more subjects we obtain a reliability coefficient of at least 0.7. We note that Russian and Farsi reliability scores are low in some categories, primarily due to lack of sufficient subject rating data. However, reliability of subject ratings for metaphor question (Q1) is sufficiently high in three of the four languages we are interested in.

Dimension	English	Spanish	Russian	Farsi
Metaphor	.908	.882	.838	.606
Affect	.831	.776	.318	.798
Commonness	.744	.753	.753	.618

Table 3. Intraclass correlations for linguistic metaphor assessment by Mechanical Turk subjects (Task 1)

4.3 Results

In Table 4, we show our performance at classifying metaphors across four different languages. The baseline in this table assigns all given examples in the test set to be metaphorical. We note that performance of the system at the linguistic metaphor level when compared to human gold standard is significantly over baseline for all four languages. The system performances cited in Table 4 validate the system against test sets that contain the distribution of metaphorical vs. literal examples as outlined in Table 5.

	English	Spanish	Russian	Farsi
Baseline	45.8%	41.7%	56.4%	50%
System	71.3%	80%	69.2%	78%

Table 4. Performance accuracy of system when compared to baseline for linguistic metaphor classification.

	English	Spanish	Russian	Farsi
Metaphor	50	50	22	25
Literal	59	70	17	25
Total	109	120	39	50

Table 5. Number of metaphorical and literal examples in test sets across all four languages.

Table 6 shows the accuracy in classification by the Affect and Force modules. We note that the low performance of affect and force for languages other than English. Our focus has been on improving NLP tools for Spanish, Russian and Farsi, so that a similar robust performance for those language can be achieved as we can demonstrate in English.

Accuracy	English	Spanish	Russian	Farsi
Affect	72%	54%	51%	40%
Force	67%	50%	33%	66%

Table 6. Affect and force performance of system on linguistic metaphor level.

5 Discussion and Future Work

In this article, we described in detail our approach to detecting metaphors in text. We have developed an automated system that does not require the existence of annotated training data or a knowledge base of predefined metaphors. We have described the various steps for detecting metaphors from receiving an input, to selecting candidate relations, to the discovery of prototypical source domains, and leading to the identification of a metaphor as well as the discovery of the potential source domain being applied in the metaphor. We presented two novel concepts that have heretofore not been fully explored in computational metaphor identification systems. The first is the exclusion of words that form the thread of the discussion in the text, by the application of a Topic Tracking module. The second is the application of Imageability scores in the selection of salient candidate relations.

Our evaluation consists first of validating the evaluation task itself. Once we ensure that sufficient reliability has been established on the various dimensions we seek to evaluate – metaphoricity, affect and force – we compare our system performance to the human gold standard. The performance of our system as compared to baseline is quite high, across all four languages of interest when measured against human assessed gold standard.

In this article, we discuss examples of metaphors belonging to a specific Target domain – "Governance". However, we can run our system through data in any domain perform the same kind of metaphor identification. In cases where the Target domain is unknown, we plan to use our Topic tracking module to recognize content words that may form part of a metaphorical phrase. This is essentially a process that is the reverse of that described in Section 3.3. We will find the salient Target concepts where there are directly dependent relations with the imageable verbs or adjectives.

In a separate larger publication, we plan to discuss in detail revisions to our Mapping module as well as the discovery and analyses of more complex conceptual metaphors. Such complex metaphors are based upon evidence from one or more instance of linguistic metaphors. Additional modules would recognize the manifold mappings, affect and force associated with the complex conceptual metaphors.

Acknowledgments

This research is supported by the Intelligence Advanced Research Projects Activity (IARPA) via Department of

Defense US Army Research Laboratory contract number W911NF-12-C-0024. The U.S. Government is authorized to reproduce and distribute reprints for Governmental purposes notwithstanding any copyright annotation thereon. Disclaimer: The views and conclusions contained herein are those of the authors and should not be interpreted as necessarily representing the official policies or endorsements, either expressed or implied, of IARPA, DoD/ARL, or the U.S. Government.

References

Allbritton, David W., Gail McKoon, and Richard J. Gerrig. 1995. Metaphor-Based Schemas and Text Representations: Making Connections Through Conceptual Metaphors, *Journal of Experimental Psychology*: Learning, Memory, and Cognition, Vol. 21, No. 3, pp. 612-625.

Baumer, Erik. P.S., White, James., Tomlinson, Bill. 2010. Comparing Semantic Role Labeling with Typed Dependency *Parsing in Computational Metaphor Identification. Proceedings of the NAACL HLT 2010 Second Workshop on Computational Approaches to Linguistic Creativity, pages 14–22,* Los Angeles, California, June 2010.

Bradley, M.M. & Lang, P.J. 2010. Affective Norms for English Words (ANEW): Instruction manual and affective ratings. Technical Report C-2. University of Florida, Gainesville, FL.

Broadwell George A., Jennifer Stromer-Galley, Tomek Strzalkowski, Samira Shaikh, Sarah Taylor, Umit Boz, Alana Elia, Laura Jiao, Ting Liu and Nick Webb. 2012. Modeling Socio-Cultural Phenomena in Discourse. *Journal of Natural Language Engineering, Cambridge Press.*

Broadwell, George A., Umit Boz, Ignacio Cases, Tomek Strzalkowski, Laurie Feldman, Sarah Taylor, Samira Shaikh, Ting Liu, Kit Cho, aand Nick Webb. 2013. Using imageability and topic chaining to locate metaphors in linguistic corpora. in Ariel M. Greenberg, William G. Kennedy, Nathan D. Bos and Stephen Marcus, eds. *Proceedings of the 6th International Conference on Social Computing, Behavioral-Cultural Modeling and Prediction SBP 2013.*

Carbonell, Jaime. 1980. Metaphor: a key to extensible semantic analysis. *Proceedings of the 18th Annual Meeting on Association for Computational Linguistics.*

Charteris-Black, Jonathan 2002 Second Language Figurative Proficiency: A Comparative Study of Malay and English. *Applied Linguistics* 23/1: 104-133.

Coltheart, M. 1981. The MRC Psycholinguistic Database. *Quarterly Journal of Experimental Psychology*, 33A, 497-505.

Fass, Dan. 1991. met*: A Method for Discriminating Metonymy and Metaphor by Computer. *Computational Linguistics, Vol 17:49-90*

Feldman, J. and S. Narayanan. 2004. Embodied meaning in a neural theory of language. *Brain and Language*, 89(2):385–392.

Fellbaum, C. editor. 1998. WordNet: An Electronic Lexical Database (ISBN: 0-262-06197-X). MIT Press, first edition.

Gedigian, M., Bryant, J., Narayanan, S., & Ciric, B. (2006). Catching Metaphors. *Proceedings of the Third Workshop on Scalable Natural Language Understanding ScaNaLU 06* (pp. 41-48). Association for Computational Linguistics.

Klein, Dan and Manning, Christoper D. 2003. Accurate Unlexicalized Parsing. *Proceedings of the 41st Meeting of the Association for Computational Linguistics*, pp. 423-430.

Krishnakumaran, S. and X. Zhu. 2007. Hunting elusive metaphors using lexical resources. In Proceedings of the Workshop on Computational Approaches to Figurative Language, pages 13–20, Rochester, NY.

Lakoff, George and Johnson, Mark. 1980. *Metaphors We Live By*. University Of Chicago Press.

Lakoff, George. 2001. *Moral Politics: what Conservatives Know that Liberals Don't.* University of Chicago Press.

Malkki, Liisa. 1992. National Geographic: The Rooting of People and the Territorialization of National Identity Among Scholars and Refugees. *Society for Cultural Anthropology* 7(1):24-44

Martin, James. 1988. A Computational Theory of Metaphor. *PH.D. Dissertation*

McGraw, K. O., & Wong, S. P. 1996. Forming inferences about some intraclass correlation coefficients. *Psychological Methods, 1*(1), 30-46.

Musolff, Andreas. 2008. What can Critical Metaphor Analysis Add to the Understanding of Racist Ideology? Recent Studies of Hitler's Anti-Semitic Metaphors, Critical Approaches to Discourse Analysis across Disciplines, http://cadaad.org/ejournal, Vol. 2(2): 1-10.

O'Halloran, Kieran. 2007. Critical Discourse Analysis and the Corpus-informed Interpretation of Metaphor at the Register Level. *Oxford University Press*

Shrout, P. E., & Fleiss, J. L. 1979. Intraclass correlations: Uses in assessing rater reliability. *Psychological Bulletin, 86* (2), 420-428.

Shutova, E. 2010. Models of Metaphors in NLP. *In Proceedings of ACL 2010, Uppsala, Sweden.*

Shutova, E. and S. Teufel. 2010a. Metaphor corpus annotated for source - target domain mappings. *In Proceedings of LREC 2010, Malta.*

Shutova, E., T. Van de Cruys and A. Korhonen. 2012. *Unsupervised Metaphor Paraphrasing Using a Vector Space Model*, In Proceedings of COLING 2012, Mumbai, India

Turney, Peter., Yair Neuman, Dan Assaf, and Yohai Cohen. 2011. Literal and metaphorical sense identification through concrete and abstract context. In Proceedings of EMNLP, pages 680–690, Edinburgh, UK

Wilks, Yorick. 1975. Preference semantics. *Formal Semantics of Natural Language*, E. L. Keenan, Ed. Cambridge University Press, Cambridge, U.K., 329--348.

Wilson, M.D. (1988) The MRC Psycholinguistic Database: Machine Readable Dictionary, Version 2. *Behavioural Research Methods, Instruments and Computers, 20(1), 6-11.*

Annotating a Russian corpus of conceptual metaphor: a bottom-up approach

Yulia Badryzlova
Urals State Pedagogical University
Prospekt Kosmonavtov 26
620034 Yekaterinburg, Russia
yuliya.badryzlova@gmail.com

Natalia Shekhtman
Urals State Pedagogical University
Prospekt Kosmonavtov 26
620034 Yekaterinburg, Russia
natalia.sh2@gmail.com

Yekaterina Isaeva
Perm State National Research University
Ul. Bukireva 15
614990 Perm, Russia
ekaterinaisae@gmail.com

Ruslan Kerimov
Kemerovo State University
Ul. Krasnaya 6
650043 Kemerovo, Russia
kerimovrus@mail.ru

Abstract

This work presents the tentative version of the protocol designed for annotation of a Russian metaphor corpus using the rapid annotation tool BRAT.

The first part of the article is devoted to the procedure of "shallow" annotation in which metaphor-related words are identified according to a slightly modified version of the MIPVU procedure. The paper presents the results of two reliability tests and the measures of inter-annotator agreement obtained in them. Further on, the article gives a brief account of the linguistic problems that were encountered in adapting MIPVU to Russian. The rest of the first part describes the classes of metaphor-related words and the rules of their annotation with BRAT. The examples of annotation show how the visualization functionalities of BRAT allow the researcher to describe the multifaceted nature of metaphor related words and the complexity of their relations.

The second part of the paper speaks about the annotation of conceptual metaphors (the "deep" annotation), where formulations of conceptual metaphors are inferred from the basic and contextual meanings of metaphor-related words from the "shallow" annotation, which is expected to make the metaphor formulation process more controllable.

1 Introduction

The manually annotated Russian-language metaphor corpus is an ongoing project in its initial stage, in which a group of native Russian experts aims to annotate a corpus of contemporary Russian texts.

The annotation is performed at the two levels:

1) shallow annotation – identification of metaphor-related words according to a slightly modified version of MIPVU, the procedure for linguistic metaphor identification (Steen et al., 2010);

2) deep annotation – identification of cross-domain mappings and formulation of conceptual metaphors on the basis of basic and contextual meanings of metaphor-related words.

The annotations are visualized with the BRAT annotation tool (http://brat.nlplab.org/, Stenetorp et al., 2012).

2. Shallow annotation

The shallow annotation, based on the MIPVU procedure for linguistic metaphor identification (Steen et al., 2010), consists in indentifying and annotating all metaphor-related words in the corpus.

2.1 MIPVU procedure

In MIPVU, **metaphor-related words** are the words whose contextual meanings are opposed to their basic meanings.

The **basic meaning** of a word is:

a) more concrete; what it evokes is easier to imagine, see, hear, feel, smell and taste;

b) related to bodily action;

c) more precise (as opposed to vague) (ibid.).

Reliability Test 1: 4 texts, 3 annotators	Reliability Test 2: 4 texts, 3 annotators	Fleiss' kappa: accepted reliable minimum	VU Amsterdam Metaphor Corpus: 4 texts, 4 annotators	VU Amsterdam Metaphor Corpus: 3 texts, 4 annotators
0.68	0.90	0.7	0.85-0.86	0.88

Table 1. Inter-annotator agreement (Fleiss' kappa) in Reliability Tests 1 and 2

The **contextual meaning** of a word is the meaning observed in a given context.

Annotators establish the basic and the contextual meaning for each word in the corpus using dictionary definitions from (Dictionary of the Russian Language, 1981-1984) which is the primary dictionary, and (Dictionary of the Russian Language, 1999) as a subsidiary dictionary.

According to MIPVU, a lexical unit is annotated as a **metaphor-related word** if its contextual meaning contrasts with its basic meaning (by the basis of concreteness, body-relatedness and preciseness, as described above), and the contextual and the basic meanings can be understood in comparison with each other: **CM⇔BM**.

A lexical unit is not a metaphor-related word if its contextual meaning is the same as its basic meaning, or if the contrast by the basis of concreteness, body-relatedness and preciseness is not conspicuous enough: **CM=BM**.

MIPVU does not take into account the historical aspect, i.e. it does not differentiate between older and newer meanings or look into the etymology of words, and treats all meanings from the standpoint of an average contemporary user of the language (Steen et al., 2010).

In BRAT annotation tool, the contextual and the basic meanings of metaphor-related words are recorded in a special text field which is displayed when a viewer hovers the computer mouse over a word.

2.2. Reliability Tests

We have performed two Reliability Tests in order to 1) to check the transferability and applicability of MIPVU, which was originally designed for English, to Russian-language material and 2) to assess the reliability of MIPVU on Russian-language material by measuring the rate of inter-annotator agreement.

The Reliability Tests had the following setup:

– 3 annotators (PhDs and current PhD students with prior experience in conceptual metaphor studies);

– a collection of 4 text excerpts (500-600 words each), representing the 4 genres: fiction, transcribed spoken, popular science/academic, and news texts;

– POS-tagged files from the National Russian Corpus (http://ruscorpora.ru/) in xhtml-format;

– 2 dictionaries used to define the word meanings: (Dictionary of the Russian Language, 1981-1984, Dictionary of the Russian Language, 1999).

The inter-annotator agreement was measured by Fleiss' kappa (Artstein and Poesio, 2008) using binary classification, i.e. 1 for any metaphor-related word and 0 for otherwise. The measure of Fleiss' kappa in Reliability Tests 1 and 2 is presented in Table 1 in comparison with the similar tests done for VUAMC, the VU Amsterdam Metaphor Corpus (Steen et al., 2010).

In the first Reliability Test, the annotators were instructed to follow the basic rules of MIPVU, as described in 2.1. As seen from Table 1, the resultant agreement was below both the inter-annotator agreement observed on VUAMC and the minimum threshold accepted for Fleiss' kappa.

Following Reliability Test 1, we analyzed the cases of disagreement between the annotators, and the reports from the annotators about the difficulties they experienced when applying MIPVU.

After that we designed the new version of the MIPVU rules which attempted to address those problems (see 2.3).

The second Reliability Test, which was run on a new collection, was annotated according to the revised rules. As a result, the inter-annotator agreement significantly improved, exceeding the statistical threshold for Fleiss' kappa and outperforming the agreement measures reported for VUAMC (see Table 1).

2.3. MIPVU rules: revised and extended

The analysis of the cases of disagreement and the annotators' problem reports has identified 3 major groups of difficulties. Two of them concerned the application of the MIPVU procedure in general, and one group of problems was specific for using MIPVU with Russian dictionaries on Russian texts.

The first major problem had to do with defining the basic meanings of words; the annotators reported significant difficulties in singling out one basic meaning from all the available meanings, as required by MIPVU. The solution for this problem suggests defining a group of basic meanings rather than one basic meaning, each of which shares the feature of concreteness, body-relatedness and preciseness. We have also listed the basic meanings of all major Russian prepositions, as prepositions are reported to account for 38.5-46.9% of metaphor-related words in a corpus (Steen et al., 2010) and therefore are essential for inter-annotator agreement.

The second issue concerned the treatment of idioms and proper names, for which MIPVU does not offer a comprehensive solution. In our version of annotation, we introduced special tags for these classes – Set Expression and Proper Name (see 2.4.6, 2.4.7).

The most numerous group of problems dealt with using Russian dictionaries and adjusting MIPVU to the specific morphological, grammatical, etc. features of Russian, such as:

- In the dictionaries, word meanings are often defined through the meanings of words that have the same morphological root, but belong to a different part of speech (deverbal nouns, adjectival participles and adverbs, adverbs formed on the basis of adverbial participles).
- Some of the meanings of imperfecitve verbs are defined on the basis of their perfective counterparts. Some of the meanings of passive verbs are defined on the basis of their active counterparts.
- Homonymous grammatical forms belonging to different parts of speech are listed in one dictionary entry.
- Agglutinative and abbreviated compound words (consisting of more than one stem) require separate analysis of each of their stems.
- Specialist terms and slang words are not listed in general dictionaries.
- The best candidate for the basic meaning may be a stylistically marked meaning of a word.

The solutions we offered to address these linguistic issues of MIPVU adaptation to Russian are described in detail in (Badryzlova et al., 2013).

2.4. Classes of metaphor-related words in the shallow annotation

Depending on the type of relation between the contextual meaning and the basic meaning, the shallow annotation of the Russian metaphor corpus distinguishes the following classes of metaphor-related words that were present in the original MIPVU procedure (Steen et al., 2010): Indirect Metaphor, borderline cases, or WIDLII (When in Doubt, Leave It In), Implicit Metaphors, Direct Metaphors, Metaphor Flags (mFlag), Personification, and lexical units discarded for metaphor analysis (DFMA). Additionally, we annotate the classes of Set Expression and Proper Name.

Importantly, the functionalities provided by BRAT annotation tool allow assigning multiple tags to a lexical unit; for example, a word or a phrase can take the tags of Indirect Metaphor and Personifier/Personified at the same time (e.g. see the word "*liniya*" in Fig. 3); metaphor-related annotations can overlap, thus displaying the multi-faceted nature of metaphor-related words and the complexity of their relations.

2.4.1 Indirect Metaphor

Indirect Metaphor is observed when the contextual meaning of a lexical unit contrasts with its basic meaning: **CM** ⇔ **BM** (Steen et al., 2010).

Figure 1: *В последнее время все чаще выпускают полноприводные машины, в которых раздаточная коробка вообще не предусмотрена.* [Recently, all-wheel drive vehicles have been produced ("released") which feature no transfer case at all.]

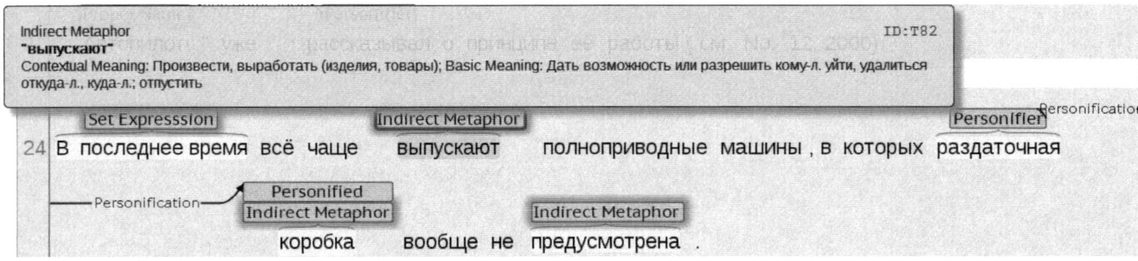

Figure 1. Indirect Metaphor

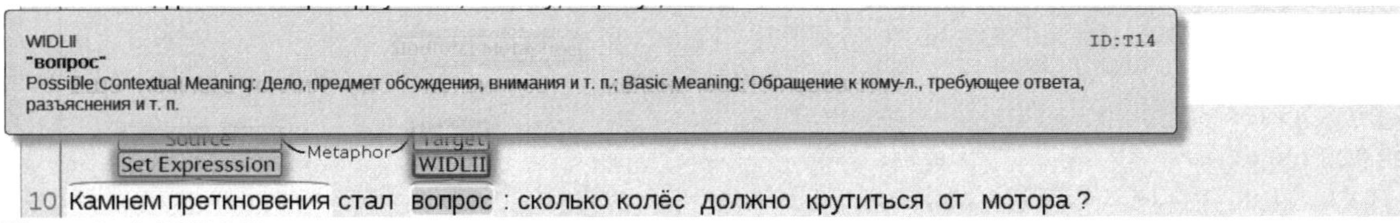

Figure 2. A WIDLII case

The verb *"vypuskat'"* in Figure 1 is an Indirect Metaphor because CM ⇔ BM:

Contextual Meaning *"vypuskat'"*		**Basic Meaning *"vypuskat'"***
Произвести, выработать (изделия, товары) [To produce, to turn out (products, goods)]	⇔	Дать возможность или разрешить кому-л. уйти, удалиться откуда-л., куда-л.; отпустить [To allow or permit smb to leave or go out; to release smb

(The fields above the sentence lines in Figures 1-6 contain the definitions of the contextual and the basic meanings. The definitions are given according to (Dictionary of the Russian Language, 1981-1984).

2.4.2 Borderline cases (WIDLII – When In Doubt, Leave It In)

We state a WIDLII case when it is not quite clear whether the contextual and the basic are identical or not, i.e. whether CM ⇔ BM or CM = BM (Steen et al., 2010).

Figure 2: *Камнем преткновения стал вопрос: сколько же колес должно крутиться от мотора?* [The following question has become the stumbling block: how many wheels should be rotated by the engine?]

The noun *"vopros"* in Figure 2 is a WIDLII case because it simultaneously displays a dual relation between the contextual and the basic meaning: CM ⇔ BM, and CM = BM:

Contextual Meaning *"vorpos"*		**Basic Meaning *"vopros"***
Дело, предмет обсуждения, внимания и т. п. [The matter or the subject of a discussion, consideration, etc.]	⇔	Обращение к кому-л., требующее ответа, разъяснения и т. п. [An utterance requiring response, explanation, etc.]

and

Contextual Meaning *"vopros"*		**Basic Meaning *"vopros"***
Обращение к кому-л., требующее ответа, разъяснения и т. п. [An utterance requiring response, explanation, etc.]	=	Обращение к кому-л., требующее ответа, разъяснения и т. п. [An utterance requiring response, explanation, etc.]

2.4.3 Implicit Metaphor

Implicit Metaphors are anaphoric pronouns that are coreferential with a metaphor-related antecedent (Steen et al., 2010). In the shallow annotation proposed in this paper, the Implicit Metaphor and its metaphoric antecedent are connected by the relation "Coreference".

Figure 3: *Однако вопреки расчетам террористов наша линия на политическое урегулирование в Чечне, опирающаяся на поддержку чеченского народа, остается неизменной. Мы высоко ценим то понимание,*

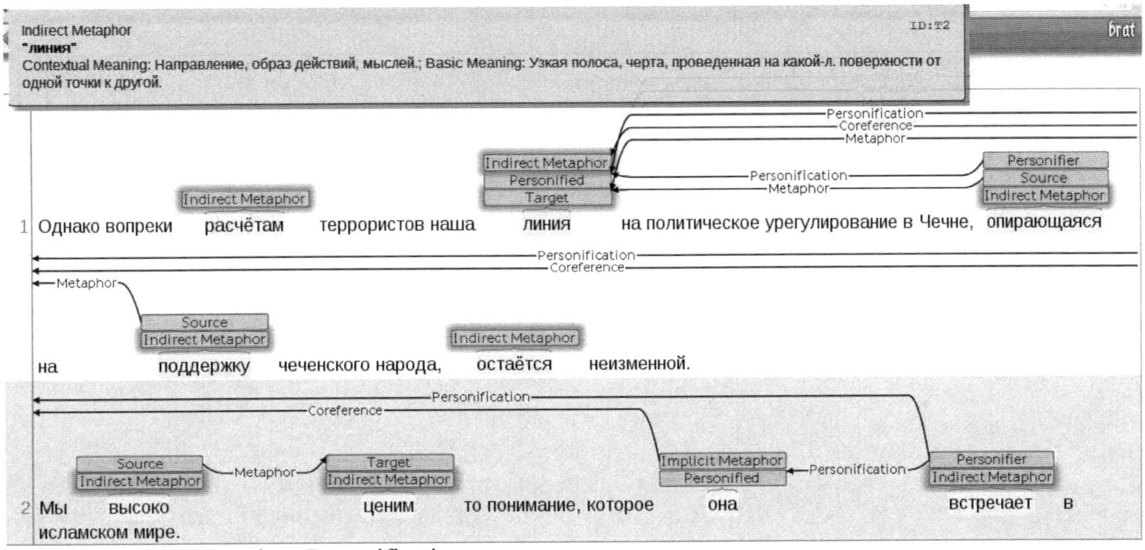

Figure 3. Implicit Metaphor, Personification

которая она встречает в исламском мире. [However, despite the expectations of the terrorists, our line on political settlement in Chechnya, which leans on the support of the Chechen people, has stayed unchanged. We highly appreciate the understanding she (it) meets in the Islamic world.]

The pronoun "*ona*" [she (it)]) in Figure 3 is an anaphor of the Indirect Metaphor "*liniya*" [line], as:

Contextual Meaning "*liniya*"		**Basic Meaning "*liniya*"**
Узкая полоса, черта, проведенная на какой-л. поверхности от одной точки к другой. [Thin mark drawn on a surface from one point to another].	⇔	Направление, образ действий, мыслей. [Direction or manner of action or thought].

Therefore, "*ona*" is a case of Implicit Metaphor.

2.4.4 Personification

We have elaborated the structure of Personification that was suggested by the original MIPVU procedure. The visualization functionalities of BRAT annotation tool have enabled us to regard personification as a relation between the two entities: the source of personification and the target of personification.

The source of personification (Personifier) is a lexical unit whose basic meaning implies the presence of an animate agent.

The target of personification (Personified) is a lexical unit denoting inanimate subjects, phenomena, or abstract notions onto which the features of an animate agent from the Personifier are mapped.

The Personifier and the Personified are connected by the relation of "Personification".

Figure 3: *Однако вопреки расчетам террористов наша линия на политическое урегулирование в Чечне, опирающаяся на поддержку чеченского народа, остается неизменной. Мы высоко ценим то понимание, которая она встречает в исламском мире.* [However, despite the expectations of the terrorists, our line on political settlement in Chechnya, which leans on the support of the Chechen people, has stayed unchanged. We highly appreciate the understanding she (it) meets in the Islamic world.]

In this sentence, already discussed above, the verb "*vstrechat'*" [to meet] (which has been tagged as Indirect Metaphor) is also the source of personification (Personifier), as its basic meaning implies an animate agent:

Contextual Meaning "*vstrechat'*"		**Basic Meaning "*vstrechat'*"**
Увидеть идущего навстречу, сойтись	⇔	Получить, испытать,

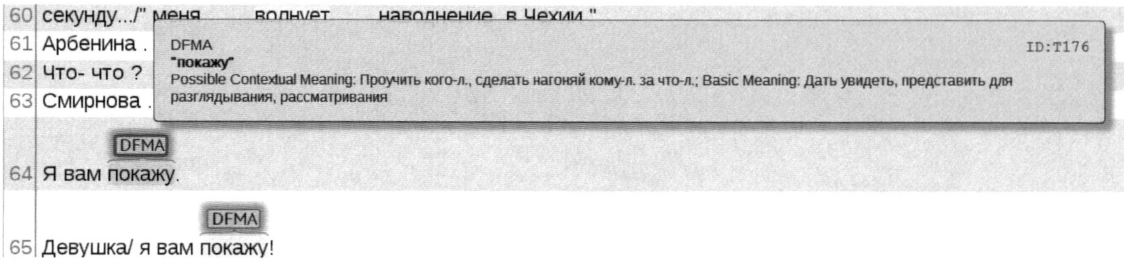

Figure 4. DFMA

с ним; Выйдя навстречу прибывающему (прибывающим), принять, приветствовать их. [To see a person walking towards you, and to approach him/her; to walk towards arriving visitor(s) while greeting and welcoming them].	оказавшись в каком-л. положении, при каком-л. действии и т. п. [To receive or experience smth while being in a certain situation, in the course of a certain action, etc.].

The target of personification (Personified) is the anaphoric pronoun "*ona*" [she] and, consequently, its metaphorical antecedent, the noun "*liniya*" [line].

2.4.5 DFMA (Discarded for Metaphor Analysis)

The tag DFMA is used in MIPVU and in our shallow annotation when the incompleteness of the context does not allow the annotator to establish the contextual meaning (Steen et al., 2010). Such cases are commonly observed either in incomplete, or syntactically, lexically or stylistically incorrect utterances that are characteristic of spoken language.

Figure 4 presents an excerpt from a TV talk show in which two female hosts interview a female rock singer: *"Смирнова. Мы/ старые тётеньки / нам нравятся ваши песни / но вот это на нас решительно не действует. Поэтому весь этот напор / и эффектное" я / космополит !"/" меня волнует..."/ как вы там сказали ... секунду.../" меня волнует наводнение в Чехии "... Арбенина. Что-что? Смирнова. Я вам покажу. Девушка/ я вам покажу!* [Host. We / old ladies / we like your songs / but these things have absolutely no effect on us / And all that drive / and the pretentious "I am / a cosmopolitan!" / "I am concerned about…" / how did you put it… just a second… / "I am concerned about the flooding in the Czech Republic"… Guest. Come again? Host. I will show you. Young lady, I will show you!]

The contextual meaning of the verb "*pokazat'*" [to show] is not apparent from the context. It is possible that the host indeed intends to demonstrate a certain object to the guest; then the contextual meaning will be identical to the basic meaning:

Contextual Meaning "*pokazat'*"		**Basic Meaning "*pokazat'*"**
Дать увидеть, представить для разглядывания, рассматривания [To allow smb to see smth, to present smth for display]	=	Дать увидеть, представить для разглядывания, рассматривания [To allow smb to see smth, to present smth for display]

However, it is also possible that the host's purport was somewhat different, for example:

Contextual Meaning "*pokazat'*"		**Basic Meaning "*pokazat'*"**
Проучить кого-л., сделать нагоняй кому-л. за что-л. [To call smb to task, to tell smb off]	⇔	Дать увидеть, представить для разглядывания, рассматривания [To allow smb to see smth, to present smth for display]

After all, in the absence of the extra-linguistic context, the available linguistic context does not appear sufficient for making a judgment about the speaker's actual intention, so the case of "*pokazat'*" is discarded for metaphor analysis.

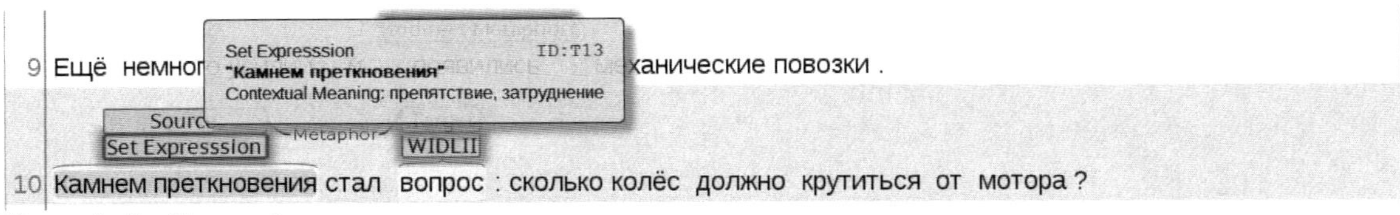

Figure 5. Set Expression

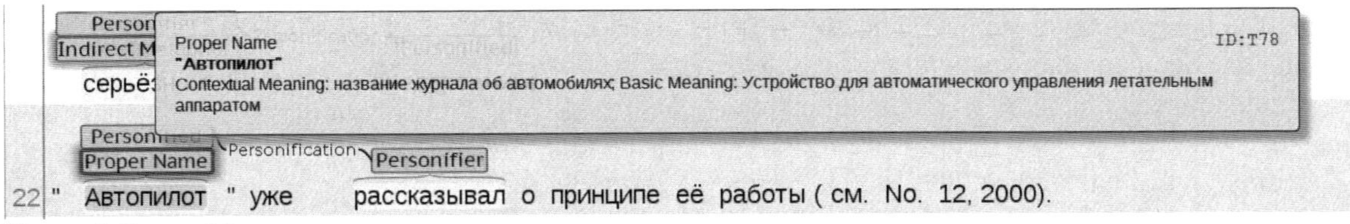

Figure 6. Proper Name

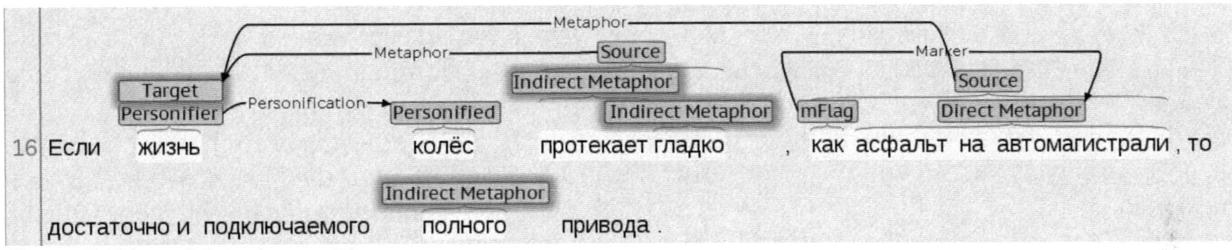

Figure 7. Direct Metaphor, mFlag

2.4.6 Set Expression

This class, initially not present in the original version of MIPVU, was introduced by us into the shallow annotation as a solution to insufficient guidelines on treatment of idiomatic expressions in MIPVU (see 2.3).

The class of Set Expressions includes idioms and multi-word units as they are listed in the dictionary. Set Expressions present a special case for metaphor analysis as semantically inseparable units with various degree of internal semantic motivation. The dictionary definition of a Set Expression in annotation is recorded as its contextual meaning.

Figure 5: *Камнем преткновения стал вопрос: сколько же колес должно крутиться от мотора?* [The following question has become the stumbling block: how many wheels should be rotated by the engine?]

The phrase "*kamen' pretknoveniya*" [stumbling block] in Figure 5 is a Set Expression whose contextual meaning is: *Препятствие, затруднение* [Hindrance, complication].

2.4.7 Proper Name

The class of Proper Names, which was not present in the original version of MIPVU, was added to our tagset in order to offer a solution to the treatment of proper names in the shallow annotation.

Proper names that have common nouns, adjectives etc. among their constituents are similar to Indirect Metaphors in that the contextual meaning contrasts the basic meaning; the difference is that the contextual meanings of proper names are normally not listed in dictionaries.

In Figure 6, the noun "*avtopilot*" is the title of an automotive magazine, which is its contextual meaning. At the same time, the basic meaning of the corresponding common noun is that of a technical device:

Contextual Meaning "*avtopilot*"		**Basic Meaning "*avtopilot*"**
Название журнала об автомобилях [Title of an automotive magazine]	⇔	Устройство для автоматического управления летательным аппаратом [Device for automatic control of an aircraft]

2.4.8 Direct Metaphor

According to MIPVU, the contextual meaning of a Direct Metaphor is identical to its basic meaning (CM = BM), and they belong to a distinctly different conceptual domain than their immediate context (Steen et al., 2010). Direct Metaphors in our annotation scheme lie on the borderline of the shallow and the deep annotation, acting as a source of cross-domain mapping.

Direct Metaphors may be introduced into the context either by means of signalling devices (metaphor flags, mFlags), or immediately, without any signalling devices (Steen et al, 2010).

Figure 7: *Если жизнь колес протекает гладко, как асфальт на автомагистрали, то достаточно и подключаемого полного привода.* [If the life of the wheels flows smoothly like asphalt on a motorway, a part-time 4-wheel-drive system will do.].

The phrase "*kak asfalt na avtomagistrali*" [like asphalt on a motorway] is a Direct Metaphor signalled by the Metaphor Flag (mFlag) "*kak*" [like]. The Metaphor Flag and the Direct Metaphor it introduces are connected by the relation "Marker".

3. Deep annotation

By deep annotation in our corpus we mean the annotation of conceptual metaphors.

We think that the coverage of conceptual metaphor identification in a corpus and the objectivity of metaphor formulation can increase to some extent if these procedures rely on the shallow annotation of metaphor-related words.

In a typical study of conceptual metaphor in discourse, annotators would a) go through a text and mark conceptual mappings, sources and targets when they feel there is a shift from one conceptual domain to another; b) assign the identified conceptual structure to a metaphor from a previously formulated list and label the Source and the Target; or they would formulate a new metaphor, Source, and Target, if they were not found in the list (e.g. Chudinov, 2001).

When we take shallow annotation as the basis for conceptual metaphor identification, a substantial component of linguistic intuition remains, as step (a) basically does not change. However, the coverage is likely to increase, because annotators would examine each metaphor-related word in the shallow annotation and assess their potential for triggering a conceptual mapping, which arises from the nature and extent of the contrast between the basic and the contextual meanings.

The objectivity of assigning conceptual metaphors to the mappings may also be expected to increase, because definitions of metaphors would be based on the dictionary definitions of the basic and the contextual meanings of metaphor-related words (MRWs). In our annotation, the inferred conceptual metaphors are recorded in the field "Possible Inferences" of the "Target" tag.

We have described several most frequent scenarios of formulating MRW-based conceptual metaphors:

1) if the Target is a non-metaphor-related word, the definition of the Target will be expressed by the contextual meaning of the non-metaphor-related word;

2) if the Target is an Indirect Metaphor, the definition of the Target will be expressed by the contextual meaning of the Indirect Metaphor;

3) if the Source is an Indirect Metaphor, the definition of the Source will be expressed by the basic meaning of the Indirect Metaphor;

4) if either the Source or the Target is a Proper Name, the definition of the Source or the Target will be expressed by the contextual meaning of the Proper Name;

5) if either the Source or the Target is a Set Expression, the definition of the Source or the Target will be expressed by the contextual meaning of the Set Expression;

6) if the Source is a Direct Metaphor, the definition of the Source will be expressed by the Direct Metaphor itself.

For example, the noun "*liniya*" [line] in Figure 3, which in itself is an Indirect Metaphor with the contextual meaning of "Direction or manner of action or thought" is the Target for mappings from the two Sources. The first is a participle of the verb "*operet'sya*" [to lean on smth], which is tagged as an Indirect Metaphor, as:

Contextual Meaning "*operet'sya*"		**Basic Meaning "*operet'sya*"**
Найти себе поддержку в ком-,	⇔	Прислониться к кому-, чему-л.,

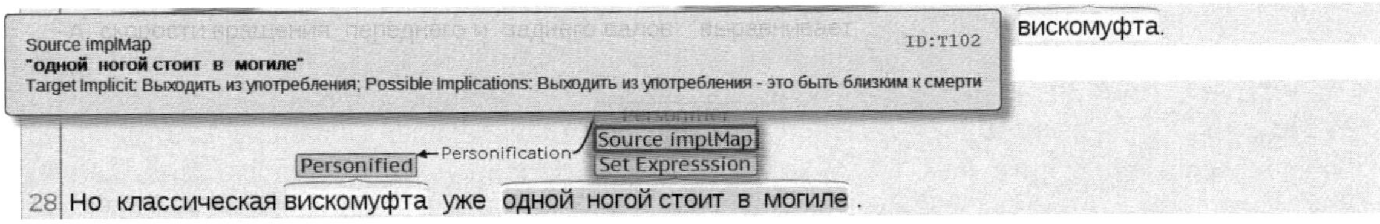

Figure 8. Explicit Source, Implicit Target and mapping

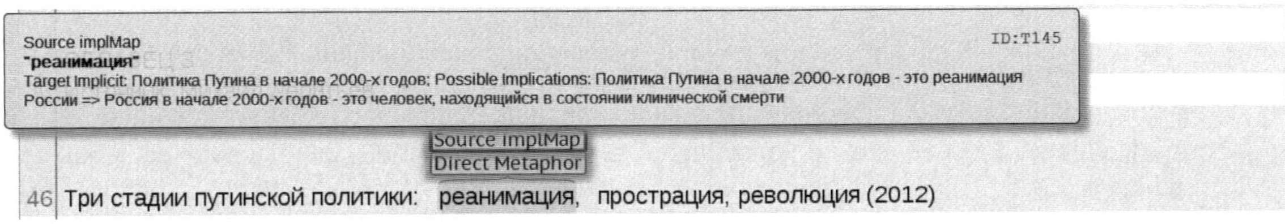

Figure 9. First- and second-order inferences

чем-л., воспользоваться кем-, чем-л. в качестве опоры, поддержки. [To find help in smb/smth, to use smb/smth as support]		налечь на кого-, что-л., перенося на него часть тяжести своего тела. [To lean against smb/smth, transferring part of your body weight onto that object]

The second Source is the noun "*podderzhka*" [support], which is also an Indirect Metaphor:

Contextual Meaning "*podderzhka*"		**Basic Meaning "*podderzhka*"**
Помощь, содействие. [help, assistance]	⇔	То, что поддерживает, служит опорой чему-л. [Smth that supports or holds the weight of smth]

The following conceptual metaphor can be inferred from these mappings and from the underlying meanings of metaphor-related words: "Direction/manner of action/thought is something that uses support to lean on or to hold its weight".

In some cases, not all the components of a conceptual metaphor may be present explicitly in the text; this happens when only the Source is expressed explicitly, while the Target and the mapping are implicit. The Implicit Target may be inferred either from the contextual meanings of the metaphor-related word(s) that express the Source, or from the topical framework of the context.

We use the tag "Source implMap" to annotate the Source of Implicit Mapping. We also record the Implicit Target in a special text field of the "Source implMap" tag, as in Figures 8-9.

Figure 8: *Но классическая вискомуфта уже одной ногой стоит в могиле.* [But the classic viscous coupling is standing with one foot in the grave]. "*Odnoy nogoy stoit v mogile*" [is standing with one foot in the grave] is a Set Expression whose contextual meaning is "To be nearing one's death". In the given context which speaks about the evolution of automotive technology, this phrase means "To come into disuse", which constitutes the Implicit Target (the Implicit Target is inferred from the topic of the context). The possible inference from the mapping of the explicit Source onto the Implicit Target may be worded as the following: "Coming into disuse is approaching one's death".

When making inferences from Source/Target mappings we have often observed that the first-order inferences that follow immediately from the metaphor-related words of the shallow level may logically entail further, second-order inferences which are also recorded in the field "Possible Inferences".

Figure 9: *(Заголовок статьи) Три стадии путинской политики: реанимация, прострация, революция.* [(Editorial headline) The three stages of Putin's policy: life support, prostration, revolution.]

"*Reanimatsiya*" [life support] is a Direct Metaphor with the basic meaning of "Actions intended to bring a person back to life from clinical death". At the same time, "*reanimatsiya*" is the Source of an Implicit Mapping, whose Implicit Target is expressed by the topic of the text, where "life support" refers to Putin's policy during his first presidential term in 2000-2004. The possible first-order inference from this mapping is: "Putin's policy in the early 2000s is life support to Russia". The possible second-order inference is: "Russia during the early 2000s is a person in the state of clinical death".

4 Conclusion

The work presented in this paper has shown that:

1) Introducing the classes of Set Expression and Proper Name has proved to be a viable solution for the insufficiency of instructions for idioms and proper names in the original version of MIPVU.
2) The visualization functionalities of BRAT annotation tool allow elaborating and expanding the structure of Implicit Metaphor (relation "Coreference" to connect the antecedent and the anaphor); of Personification (source of personification (Personifier) connected with the target of personification (Personified) by the relation "Personification"); and of Direct Metaphor (Direct Metaphor connected with Metaphor Flag by the relation "Marker"). Cross-domain mappings can be annotated as relations between the Source and the Target.
3) BRAT annotation tool enables recording and storing the basic and the contextual meanings of metaphor-related words and the conceptual metaphors inferred from them. Implicit conceptual mappings can be annotated, where only the Source is expressed explicitly.
4) Using multiple overlapping tags and relations visualized through BRAT helps reveal the complexity of the metaphoric structure of a text.
5) The attempt to identify and formulate conceptual metaphors on the basis of the basic and contextual meanings of the underlying metaphor-related words tends to lead to increased coverage and more controlled metaphor formulation.

Acknowledgements

This work has been funded by the Russian Foundation for Humanities Research/RGNF (Grant No 12-34-01269). The authors would like to thank Olga Lyashevskaya and Dmitri Sitchinava from the National Russian Corpus for making available the data from the Corpus; Yevgenia Mikhaylikova and Pavel Durandin for technical assistance; and Pavel Braslavski for valuable support and encouragement.

References

Anatoly P. Chudinov. 2001. *Russia through the mirror of metaphors: a cognitive study of political metaphor (1991-2000)*. [Rossiya v metaforicheskom zerkale: kognitivnoye issledovaniye politicheskoy metafory (1991-2000)]. Yekaterinburg, Urals State Pedagogical University.

Brat Rapid Annotation Tool, available at: http://brat.nlplab.org/.

Dictionary of the Russian Language [Slovar russkogo yazyka]. 1981-1984. Ed. Anastasia P. Yevgenyeva. Moscow, Russkiy Yazyk, available at: http://slovari.ru/

Dictionary of the Russian Language [Tolkovyy slovar russkogo yazyka]. 1999. Eds. Sergey I. Ozhegov and Natalia Yu. Shvedova. Moscow, Azbukovnik, available at: http://slovari.ru/

Gerard J. Steen, Aletta G. Dorst, J. Berenike Herrmann, Anna A. Kaal, Tina Krennmayr and Trijntje Pasma. 2010. *A method for linguistic metaphor identification: From MIP to MIPVU*. Amsterdam, John Benjamins.

Pontus Stenetorp, Sampo Pyysalo, Goran Topić, Tomoko Ohta, Sophia Ananiadou and Jun'ichi Tsujii. 2012. Brat: a Web-based Tool for NLP-Assisted Text Annotation. *Proceedings of the Demonstrations Session at EACL 2012* (102-107). Avignon, France: 13th Conference of the European Chapter of the Association for computational Linguistics.

Ron Arstein and Massimo Poesio. 2008. Inter-coder agreement for computational linguistics. *Computational Linguistics*, 34(4) (554-596).

The Russian National Corpus [Natsionalyy Korpus Russkogo Yazyka], available at: http://ruscorpora.ru/

VU Amsterdam Metaphor Corpus, available at: http://ota.ahds.ac.uk/headers/2541.xml

Yulia Badryzlova, Natalia Shekhtman, Yekaterina Isaeva and Ruslan Kerimov. 2013. Using the linguistic metaphor identification procedure (MIPVU) on a Russian corpus: rules revised and extended (Manuscript in preparation).

Author Index

Association for Computational Linguistics
209 N. Eighth Street
Stroudsburg, Pennsylvania 18360